# LIBATION

# LIBATION

## – A Bitter Alchemy –

## DEIRDRE HEEKIN

Chelsea Green Publishing
White River Junction, Vermont

Project Manager: Emily Foote
Developmental Editor: Ben Watson
Copy Editor: Laura Jorstad
Proofreader: Helen Walden
Designer: Peter Holm,
        Sterling Hill Productions

Printed in the United States of America
First printing April, 2009
10 9 8 7 6 5 4 3 2 1  09 10 11 12 13

**Our Commitment to Green Publishing**
Chelsea Green sees publishing as a tool for cultural change and ecological stewardship.
We strive to align our book manufacturing practices with our editorial mission and to
reduce the impact of our business enterprise in the environment. We print our books and
catalogs on chlorine-free recycled paper, using vegetable-based inks whenever possible.
This book may cost slightly more because we use recycled paper, and we hope you'll agree
that it's worth it. Chelsea Green is a member of the Green Press Initiative (www.greenpres-
sinitiative.org), a nonprofit coalition of publishers, manufacturers, and authors working to
protect the world's endangered forests and conserve natural resources. *Libation, A Bitter
Alchemy,* was printed on Natures Book Natural, a 30-percent postconsumer recycled paper
supplied by Thomson-Shore.

Library of Congress Cataloging-in-Publication Data

Heekin, Deirdre.
  Libation : a bitter alchemy / Deirdre Heekin.
    p. cm.
  ISBN 978-1-60358-086-1
  1.  Heekin, Deirdre--Anecdotes. 2.  Wine and wine making--Anecdotes. 3.  Vinters--
Vermont--Anecdotes. I. Title.

 TP548.H34 2009
 641.2--dc22

                              2009008246

Chelsea Green Publishing Company
Post Office Box 428
White River Junction, VT 05001
(802) 295-6300
www.chelseagreen.com

*Drink deep, or taste not.*
ALEXANDER POPE

# — contents —

# — preface —

Winter has arrived. Eight inches of snow disguise the once green summer fields out my windows. From where I sit inside, the matte quality of the gray daylight obscures what I know to be a slick glaze of ice coating the snow. The sky is only a shade darker than the ground, tone on tone marked by the spindly branches of bare trees and a marching line of young, single grapevines making a variegated black lace along the gentle slope of hill and meadow in the near distance. Smoke from the chimneys of neighboring houses hangs in the air. The weather forecast calls for more snow.

I sit at my dining room table with a stack of wine books. Scattered about me on the surface are a compilation of winemakers' newsletters, a geographic map of our land, a soil survey, and—attached to little plastic sacks— the directions for putting together a proper soil sample. A notebook I've been keeping, whose light brown pulp paper cover is stained with circles of wine from the feet of tasting glasses, is open, and I review my notations from my first year of making wine. In the margin, I can see the word *libation* written as if I meant it as a possible name for the label on my wine. Series of definitions are hastily scrawled beneath: an intoxicating beverage; the act of drinking an intoxicating beverage; a taste of food or drink taken at a meal; a ritual pouring of a drink. In ancient Greece, a libation of precious liquid would be offered at the altar: perfumes, wine, honey, milk, oil, or fruit juice. Libations composed of barley, wine, honey, and water were used to summon the shades in Hades. This is noted in Homer's *Odyssey*. In many cultures, a libation is poured on the ground as an offering back to the earth, an acknowledgment of one's history, or in remembrance of the dead.

In the winemaking notes themselves, I compare procedures and mistakes from one year to the next. If you'd asked me twenty years ago what I would be doing far into the future, I would never have guessed that I would try my hand at fermenting grapes into wine.

Seventeen years ago, my husband, Caleb, and I married on a hot September Saturday, then traveled abroad the next day with two large duffel bags, one-way tickets, and a desire for the unexpected. I've told this story before, and because it is a story of our awakening, I will tell it many times again. We lived in Italy for a year, a complicated yet propitious year that would alter the course of our lives. There, we taught dance lessons to local beauties in an old Baroque church converted into a gymnasium, gave English classes to unruly Italian ten-year-olds at the local American exchange program. We pulled beers and mixed cocktails at a new piano bar in a cellar that once hid Jews during World War II, the same piano bar where we learned our rather colorful barroom Italian. That year, we ate and drank simply and exceedingly well. We tasted something different yet familiar; the words for what we were experiencing, like a forgotten memory, were elusive but there just out of reach somewhere on the tips of our tongues.

Five years later, after other extended trips between the States and our adoptive culture in Italy, the words for which we had been searching found their expression. Caleb and I would open a little bakery and restaurant in a small town in Vermont, which we christened Pane e Salute, bread and health, after a sliver of a bakery we used to frequent in Italy. Our Pane e Salute became a collage of all those tastes, images, scents, and sounds that had so shaped our vision.

After a time, the bakery morphed and became subsumed completely by the restaurant. Caleb and I found our own intentions with which to fashion this joint adventure: Caleb creates dishes from heirloom Italian recipes that we've collected over the years, using the raw materials grown and raised in and on our Vermont *terroir,* both cultivated and wild-gathered; I assemble an archive of rare and indigenous wine varietals from Italy based on taste and scent, history and future. Together, we try to build menus of flavor, geography, and recollection.

For me, in my effort to understand better my work tasting and pairing wine, I have been drawn to the physicality of actually making wine. Yet my introduction to making wine has been through the world of spirits, as liqueurs seemed possible efforts whereas wine always seemed too mysterious and complex. The leap to making wine became less overwhelming, however, after years of creating infusions out of fruit, flowers, spices, and brandy. Still, learning the mechanics only of the *cantina,* or "wine cellar," have not been enough. As a believer that truly good wine is made in the vineyard, I've wanted my own grapes in my own soil to tend. Vermont seems an unlikely place and climate to grow grapes and make wine, but I am an unlikely winemaker.

Yet, on further reflection, Vermont is not as improbable as one might think. Wild grapes run rampant in our side road thickets, wild grapes that we pick to bake into flatbread with rosemary and anise seeds, or roast with sausages and onions. Our northern clime skirts on the edge of a burgeoning national winemaking culture, and I have always been attracted to the fringe, the underdog, the impossible, the come-from-behind hero. Vermont currently boasts around twenty vineyards, that number growing, all of them working with cold-hardy grapes that seem to thrive in our ledgy, silty, and even loamy soils.

This book is about soil, vines, fruit, history, scent, taste, chemistry, and memory. This is a memoir in the strictest sense of the word, comprising linked essays that explore my own development of nose and palate. I've tried to set down the stories of the personalities and landscapes that have shaped my ongoing education and relationship with wine and spirits. Intercutting the essays are a series of entries that follow my first attempts at planting grapes— some failed, some miraculous—and at making wine in the improbable location of northern New England. These sections, a naive winemaker's diary of sorts labeled *Work, Progress*, are not a definitive guide to successful winemaking, but I do hope to provide some practical thoughts as well as cautionary notes from my own errors, and to have the overall experience of these pages—these essays and diary—be one of agreeable intoxication. I offer these pages, as I will the liquid from my first bottle of wine, to the ground and landscape that have inspired me, to the memories that sculpt my own history, and to those who have gone fiercely and bravely before me. For them—this is my libation.

# LIBATION

– 1 –

*let us eat and*

Let us eat and drink; for to-morrow we shall die.

<small>Old Testament</small>

*I* wish I could tell you that I've got alcohol in my—well, not in my blood exactly, but in my DNA. I wish I could trace my family history back to vocational winemakers from Italy, or France, or even California; a story replete with a derelict château, or a sprawling stone farmhouse famous in the village for its perfectly cool cellars, redolent of lime and metal. If only my grandparents or great-grandparents had come through the port of Naples, sleeping on lice-infested mats in the ship's hold, holding tight to their dear wooden chest of seeds and vines, planting a vineyard in a New World row-house garden once they'd found work and lodging. I'd like to tell you how I played in the afternoons as a child under a raw-hewn pergola draped with ripening grapes, and how a grandfather showed me how to prune the vines, pick the fruit, and cleverly extract the essence, so that the family could have glasses filled with rough ruby or tawny bronze at Christmas and the New Year.

I would even settle for a tale of my ancestor's still, since I come from points south, meaning *the* South. Could I conjure up an ill-begotten contraption that smoked and churned as the family made their private label by the shine of a midnight moon? Or a story of a mad professor uncle from New Orleans whose claim to notoriety was his ingenuity with wormwood; the maker of a first-rate absinthe who died from the fruits of his own labors before he could be enshrined by provincial history?

Such stories, as beguiling as I might find them, are not *my* story. I cannot say I have come by my passion honestly. Rather, I find myself holding up a glass to the light, recommending a vintage, planting a vine, tasting a rare liqueur, all because my path forked from my ancestral road.

I come from a long line of drinkers. Not just good-time, good ol' boy or good ol' girl high-living lovers of spirits—but serious, intoxicated, obsessive drinkers. In my history, there are morality tales of distended livers, ruined beauty, unrealized potential, broken bones, angry mothers, absent (yet charming) fathers, rootless wanderers, and early graves. This often dark lineage makes up branches and trunk of my family tree.

These drinkers and their relations always thought they had enough control to keep the fixation within the confines of the home. But try as any clan might, they had no luck in keeping secrets. By the end of the story, their skeletons always came tumbling out—not dancing from joy at being released, but staring with wide, surprised eyes into the too-bright light.

Perhaps a psychoanalyst would say that my work with spirits is "noxious," that I should turn my attention to something less risky for someone of my genetic constitution. But I've been eager to redress all that went before. I want my story to be one of redemption.

The day after I was married, and my husband, Caleb, and I flew to Italy on those one-way tickets and took up residence in a small village for a year, the hospitality and generosity we found in a place so far away from home changed all our best-laid plans. We were blindsided by the unexpected. Our honeymoon gave us our vocation. We found much of what we were looking for, not just on numerous plates of home-spun dishes made in narrow, modest kitchens, but in short tumblers of local wine. That wine was made from vineyards we had walked through before harvest, stealing handfuls of grapes along the way. The world of wine and spirits changed for me in that foreign place, and continues to change as Italy becomes less and less foreign to me, for now Italy has become my second, my adoptive home.

I remember the moment of my conversion clearly. Really it is two moments that have blended into one, as two sides of one coin. The first is a simple, almost banal experience. It is Italy's early autumn, rainy and damp outside. It has to be Monday (because the piano bar is closed on Mondays), and we've traveled almost an hour from our village of Castiglion Fiorentino to our friend Gianfranco's family's village not far from Florence. The air smells like wet stone, and the damp gets under our clothes and under our skin and seeps into our bones. I am constantly trying to get warm. We weave our way through the slender little alleys of the old Ponte agli Stolli and up a flight of stone stairs to the family apartment. The kitchen is small, but there is room for a table with six chairs near the stove. Gianfranco's mother, Palmira, is making lunch, a simple pasta served with a ragu made from last night's braised rabbit, some carrots, an onion, and a hint of tomato. Gianfranco's brother-in-law's father, his health poor, sleeps in a room off the kitchen. His maternal grandmother, Angelina, sits at the table with us.

My husband and I haven't been in Italy long, but we have recently gone with Gianfranco to move Angelina from the house in which she was born in Umbria. Angelina is petite, but to me she is grand. All I know about her is that she is considered to have magical powers; she is revered for her abilities in removing and dealing with the *malocchio,* or Evil Eye. I am fascinated and almost credulous.

One rather bright light hangs from the kitchen ceiling. The floor is terra-cotta, and the walls are covered with brown and beige tile. The kitchen cabinets are dark wood, and the kitchen table is covered in a plastic tablecloth with a repeating pattern of sheaves of wheat. The chairs, typically Tuscan, are rush-seated. The kitchen window that looks out over the overgrown hillside steams up from the boiling water on the stove. While we wait for the pasta to cook, we start with fresh sheep's-milk ricotta, still warm and draining in its basket. We eat it with *pane sciocco,* the saltless Tuscan bread, the plain foil to the intensity of seasonings in the cured meats and roasted dishes typical in Tuscan cuisine.

A green-glass water bottle is on the table, but instead of being filled with water it holds local wine. We have short, narrow glasses, and we fill them as the wine goes around the table. Its pale red roughness has been cut with a little sparkling water. This dilution is usual, traditional even. Economical. My first experience with local wine in Italy is not from a vaunted, aged bottle of brilliance. This is honest, unpretentious wine.

The second defining moment happens only a few weeks later, but this time the meal we share with Gianfranco's family is in the small restaurant dining room that they run only on weekends. This kitchen and dining room are where we've had many firsts: our first meal in Italy; our first Tuscan pizza, our first dish of small, roasted birds; our first attempt at making pasta; our first lighting of the kitchen's tiny beehive oven. We are gathered on November 1 for All Saints' Day, a holiday in Italy on par with our American Thanksgiving. All the tables in the restaurant have been put together to make one long surface. The menu is epic. There are crostini (those little toasts topped with brightly flavored tapenades). There are platters of cured meats, fresh and aged cheeses. There are two pastas, one a penne with cooked tomato, onion, and pancetta; the other is made of long fresh noodles glistening in olive oil and flecked with prized black truffles. There is roasted chicken and roasted pork. There are *uccellini* (roasted little birds like squab) lending a pronounced earthiness to all the previous tastes. Then comes fish roasted in salt and rosemary. After these courses there arrive the side dishes and salads. Dessert is a decadent tray of cream-filled pastries from the *pasticceria*.

The wine throughout the meal is still local, but a bigger

expression of the hills surrounding us. It's darker and muskier and served full-strength—only the elderly at the table cut it with sparkling water. After the meal there is time for a rest, then we go out into the oblique afternoon sun for a walk in the countryside, our destination an abandoned village. Who could believe that a nap and fresh air would render us hungry again? But we are, and we pluck to eat on the walk what nature offers us: rose hips, fresh figs, and grapes on unharvested vines.

It was there at those two tables, and during our afternoon sojourn in the land that produced our meals, that I learned that wine is not something to be separated from daily living. Wine is food. I learned of its integrity to the Italian feast. Wine is an element in the experience just like spices or herbs are an element to a dish. This holds true for all spirits in Italy. From the *aperitivo,* concoctions made from Campari or Prosecco to whet the appetite; to *caffé corretto,* espresso laced with grappa or whisky; and to *digestivi,* the post-prandial elixirs specific to regions, towns, villages, and individual homes and families. Wine and spirits complement the food and the hours of the day; they make a thread that helps connect the narrative of life as it is lived.

In those early days of my learning about wine, I appreciated at once the profound difference of alcohol in the Italian way of life in comparison with the world in which I had grown up. New, exotic, joyful experiences supplanted disquieting memories. Once, when I was dining with my parents in a very proper, dark-paneled restaurant in Boston, I bragged with great brio that I had become known as the "Shot Queen" on my college campus, drinking every willing contender literally under the table. I was tough. Wasn't I tough? My mother practically dragged me home by the scruff of my neck. She made me swear on a small black Bible (I can still see its pages, gold-leaf-edged) that I would no longer drink in such a way. Growing up Catholic and superstitious by nature, I would never dare buck a promise made on the Holy Book.

But was renunciation agreeable? By stark contrast, in Italy, alcohol was not to be feared. In fact, for me it suddenly lost all its venom, and in so doing it lost a secretive, dark power over me. I could finally take pleasure in the full complement of all that was offered to me at the table—without fearing chaos in myself or in others. Imbibing with restraint felt natural. The restraint was not punitive, but a discipline of savoring. Could Angelina, Gianfranco's mysterious grandmother, the sorceress of those long-held shadowy traditions, have helped remove my own Evil Eye?

It seems a long time ago, those first days in that village in eastern Tuscany. I have devoted many years since to owning and running that small Vermont restaurant with my husband—a venture inspired by our "other life" abroad. Now my role has deepened and clarified as I've expanded my efforts. My role first was that of pastry chef. But two cooks in the tight kitchen meant that neither one of us was watching the front of our house, circulating and welcoming guests, guiding their choices. It was inevitable that I should move my energies to the front and manage what was initially a fledgling wine list. Ever since that shift,

I have dedicated myself to creating a temple to Italian varietals, many of them rare and almost extinct. I've felt drawn to the alchemy of all the other spirits as well. My education has been marked with trials and errors, the minor tragedies and little epiphanies of the everyday palate. I could not have told you fifteen, twenty years ago that this is where I'd be standing. The journey has been unanticipated and all the more savory for its surprise.

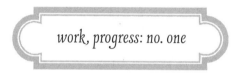

*work, progress: no. one*

A thick, dense fog rises from the disappearing snow on a December afternoon. I look out through the apple orchard between our house and perennial garden, a potager of now blackened and snow-covered roses, nepeta, scented geranium, and hydrangea lined by boxwood allowed to grow wild. I look beyond the garden, past our newly erected greenhouse or hoophouse, which protects our crop of hardy radicchio, chicory, and endive, past the little potting shed now converted to a studio and extra summer bedroom for guests. The potting shed was on the property when we bought it eleven years ago, a forlorn little red building shunted off to the side of a meadow, propped up by a stone wall. We've moved it three times, trying to find the right location, and will probably move it again. The original owners had used it to house two lambs that they bought at auction one summer. This building protected the lambs at night from the prowling coyotes that regularly cross our meadows to reach the wild terrain on a ridge above our land called the Chateauguay. Now the potting shed stores an assortment of terra-cotta pots during the winter and a rough-hewn cedar desk. Pale aqua chintz curtains culled from a village matron's salon hang at the French doors. The shed holds my ever-growing collection of wine and perfume books that I keep thinking I will box up any day now, bringing them into the house for winter reading and to keep the pages from curling with winter cold and damp.

My thoughts circle around topography, the shape and contour of our land. The meadow beyond the potting shed is open, gently sloping, and takes sun from the east and south all year long. Early on, we joked about the site being prime for growing grapes. Then we found on the edges of our meadow the thick, sinewy vines crawling and twining up poplar and maple, any tree they could get their grasping fingers around. In summer, small hard chartreuse-colored fruits would appear, and by September, if the birds had not stolen them yet, they would ripen black, and taste pungent and foxy. We pick them for cooking in fall—for making flatbread, or stewing with meats—even a hearty white fish. I consider the possibilities of a wildly cultivated dessert wine.

Since our discovery of rampant wild grapes on our hillside, we've started to believe that wine grapes could grow on the gentle slope of our meadow. So three years ago, we began an experiment. We planted two local varieties of wine grapes called Frontenac Gris and St. Croix around the house and twisting up a pergola over a terrace to see how they'd do. This year, they produced beautiful *grappole*—bunches of healthy fruits. A family of wild turkeys apparently thought they were beautiful, too, and gobbled them up before we could pick them for our own purposes. On less generous days, we think our adoptive turkeys might make a series of tasty roasts.

Looking out over the field as the early-winter sky darkens for evening, and the radio announcer warns of an imminent snowstorm, and the weatherman talks of Polaris, the North Star of our winter night sky, I consider the work that needs to be done to plant a vineyard: choosing the varietals, putting them in the ground, tending them for the three to six years until they produce fruit, then the arduous tasks of picking them carefully, pressing them into juice, fermenting, racking, fining, aging, and bottling the juice into wine. I consider the long road ahead and my lack of patience. In the end, the fruit, the juice, the wine will not be so much about the vine. It will be up to the chemistry of the earth in the meadow beyond the potting shed, that tricky and seductive notion of *terroir* that I have come to know through my work tasting and cataloging wine. In the end, planting this vineyard will be all about dirt.

–2–

*never brewed,*
*I taste a*

I taste a liquor never brewed,
from tankards scooped in pearl.
EMILY DICKINSON, "EXCLUSION"

If my relationship with wine changed when I first lived in Italy in a small village and sat in a small kitchen at a wooden table covered in oilcloth while draining pasta steamed the windows over an enamel sink, while I ate fresh sheep's-milk ricotta still warm from the farm on a Sunday afternoon, my romance with wine began several years later on the floor of my own restaurant thousands of miles away in another small village sitting on the same latitude.

When my husband and I first opened our bakery after living in Italy, I learned to make sweets like honeyed cornmeal buns and apple cakes, and I would whip up Renaissance desserts made from cream, eggs, chocolate, and almond meringue pulled from old recipe tomes that I read before bedtime. When the bakery began to change its shape, and before we understood that the bakery really wanted to become a restaurant, we began ordering wine from the local purveyors so that we had something to wash down the simple lunches we had begun to offer.

Roasted chicken on a winter day begs for a small glass of red wine, even just half a glass. A petite omelet made with fresh herbs really calls for a little Prosecco on a warm sunny day while you thankfully sit in the shade.

At the beginning, there wasn't much on offer in Vermont when it came to Italian wines. We had decided early on that, given the mission with our food—to make and offer old regional Italian dishes and sweets with the best of our local ingredients—our wine would follow suit. The wine list was naturally small; we had eight or nine, half red and half white. Rosé or a good sparkling Lambrusco were distant thoughts for the future.

As the bakery molted away, what was left was the small restaurant of our original ambition—the one in our fantasies that we shopped for every day at the market in order to find the freshest local ingredients. In our vision we had just a handful of seats, and we would name our fledgling establishment *Quello Che C'e*—What There Is—because the dishes offered would change all the time based on what was in the larder. The vision came full circle; the only difference was that we never changed the name. We kept the original from the bakery—Pane e Salute—to remind us of where we started.

As work changed, I myself changed, and no longer made desserts for our business but pored over wine portfolios and books, tasted countless wines on my own and with soon-to-be mentors, and tried to figure out what to serve with my husband's cooking.

My years of studying, an education in scent and taste, became particular in focus as I narrowed my sights to the two thousand or so varieties of wine in Italy. Even in a lifetime of study, I will never know them all. It's a relief and a satisfaction to know that I will never want for a new, intriguing taste with an intriguing history; yet there's a sadness and a poignancy to my not having enough time in life to make every varietal's acquaintance.

In the beginning, I spotted one rare varietal wine on one of my purveyors' lists. Usually, they came around peddling the chicest of Chiantis and the boldest of Barolos, both expensive haute couture little numbers. While I certainly wanted a good solid representation of these two wines on my list, my eye wandered to a wine made from a grape called Freisa in the Piemonte region of Italy. An image of sweet-scented flowers crossed my mind. I had a vague recollection of having once heard of this wine, but I knew nothing about it.

The bottle was a 1995 vintage with a grand name: Mondaccione. I bought many bottles. This was 1998, and I still have one bottle of this wine left—I am loath to open it. (My desire is to keep it as a talisman, to remind me of how I got from one place to another, but wine is meant to be drunk, and it seems sacrilege not to do just that.) The first time I tasted the wine, my husband and I were full of an electric energy, anticipating our getting to taste something almost secret. The wine was a ruby-colored crystal and smelled of fresh black raspberries and crushed violets. The taste was as light as the look and shimmied across the tongue. There was earth in the palate, a hint of cows in the barnyard telling us that this was a real wine made in a real place, a gestalt experience of the definition of *terroir*. In the thirty seconds or so that we sipped, tasted, and took in the wine, we made a journey across the world to someplace else.

I was hooked; I had a vocation. I would concentrate my energies on collecting the lesser-known regional varietals of Italy. I would fashion a wine-list-cum-living-organic-archive. I would travel to the landscapes that produced the wines, eat the food that accompanied them, learn of the people and the places that made them. I could see the shapes of grapevines in the thick blue veins jutting from the back of my hands, and I felt like a gypsy reading my own palm.

As my knowledge of the types and tastes of Italian wines grew, I understood that I needed to understand not only what poured forth from the bottle, but what came *before* the bottle. Terms like *maceration, malolactic fermentation,* and *racking* began to take on meaning. This seemed like a natural progression. In order to speak passionately about the wines I served in the restaurant, I wanted to be able to impart something of the landscape from which they came and how they were made.

When traveling to Italy and visiting vineyards, I would walk down rows of vines and take photographs of the thick, sinewy trunks, and the shape of the leaves of the early-spring growth, in order to remember them when I returned home. I would take note of the style of cultivation: *guyot, alberello,* or *trellis.*

It wasn't until the end of a dinner in a beautiful restaurant at the foot of the Aspromonte Mountains in Calabria that my efforts to know how fruit, flowers, or spices become a wine or an after-dinner *digestivo* slid me unexpectedly into thinking I could make these conconctions myself.

This small restaurant, which I will call The Piazzetta, was in a hotel owned by two brothers in the town of C--. Our trip here to Calabria was more spontaneous than some of our others. We had decided not to book places in advance but to follow our noses and the advice of locals. We found the hotel-restaurant in a little promotional book from another hotel. Here was just the place we wanted to go: small, intimate, well appointed without being fussy, with a focus on the local food and wine. We had called a couple of days in advance to ensure they had rooms. As with our arrival at so many other special places in Italy, we went through a shabby section of town, across a railroad track, then came upon this paradise with surprise.

Each room was its own little cottage with a sitting room, bedroom, and full bath. The style was modern eclectic, and the art on the walls contemporary, by local artists. There was a pool and some new landscaping. The restaurant had been in existence for a while, but the rooms were a relatively new addition. We were surrounded by lemon and orange trees, fat palms, and heavily scented oleander. The effect was intoxicating and exotic. We were encouraged to rest for the afternoon, then come to dinner later in the evening in the restaurant on the other side of the pool.

Alessandro, one of the brothers, was dressed in a beautiful pin-striped suit, his sartorial elegance topped by a stylish haircut. I noticed silver at the edges of his hair. He was maître d' and a consummate host. He seated us with a gallant flourish, gave us the menus, and proceeded to tell us about other dishes not written down before us. "We have something very special this evening that I cannot tell you about," he said with a wink. "But I highly recommend it, as it is a rarity."

Somehow alert to other hints and meanings between the lines, Caleb understood something of what Alessandro was offering, and he ordered it without hesitation. We knew it would be fish, and young.

The prized delicacy of *neonati*, unborn anchovies, arrived. At that time of year it is illegal to harvest *neonati* because of the declining population of wild-caught fish. But sometimes a female anchovy is caught with a belly full of babies, and what is a chef to do? She cannot be thrown back in the water. Why waste a good thing? It would not be responsible to do so. The dish shines black and silver like treasure and is simply dressed with lemon and olive oil. We knew everything that followed would be magic.

As I have learned, the key to fully appreciating any post-prandial drink is the meal beforehand, which serves to introduce or frame them. That night, we dined sublimely on the flavors of the local Calabrian cuisine: a plate of *maiale nero,* a cured black pork salame; little *panzerotti* stuffed with fresh ricotta made from *bufala* (water buffalo) milk and dressed with a simple sauce of wild herbs; and a fillet of *podolico,* a rare breed of cattle, in a *salsa Calabrese* made from sweet onions and fresh strawberries. For fish, we had fried big shrimp and mint with more of those delicate onions and oranges. Dessert was a simple finish of dried figs and nuts with white chocolate scented with mint.

We opted for the house *rosolio* tasting for the end of the meal. We could not pass up the opportunity to taste the five flavors offered: coffee, rose, violet, mint, and saffron. They arrived in five bottles in vibrant colors. We sipped and analyzed each, comparing them and trying to isolate their different ingredients. When Caleb went back into the kitchen to meet and talk with Alessandro's brother Mauro, the chef, I asked Alessandro about the recipes for the five *rosolii;* I wrote them down in a small notebook, imagining myself someday bringing five brightly colored elixirs to the table in my own restaurant.

Those five flavors and five bottles launched me on a circuitous path (some might call it primrose; others, golden) on which I would cross from the safe country of the appreciator into the unknown country of the maker.

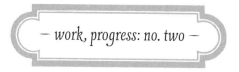

— *work, progress: no. two* —

The soil map says our particular plot of land, labeled *15C,* is from the Shelburne Series and consists of very deep, well-drained soils formed in loamy glacial till, and gently sloping to very steep soils on glaciated uplands. Technically, our land should fall in the Dummerston Series given where we are located, but the actual components of the soil suggest otherwise. The till is derived mainly from *micaceous schist* and some *siliceous limestone.* Permeability is moderate. The various *horizons,* or layers of substrata, range from strongly to moderately acid. Occasional remnants of siliceous limestone *ghosts* (fossils) are a common feature. Fine earth texture is loam, fine sandy loam, or sandy loam throughout.

I am no scientist, and certainly no geologist, but the trip to our county USDA and NRCS office is inspiring. The scientists there are welcoming and helpful, and we even know the soil specialist as a client of the restaurant, but never understood that his specialty was bedrock and marl divided by words like *oxyaquic dystrudepts, taxonomy, pedons,* and *solum.*

When Caleb and I arrive at the office, I imagine that we will be looking at old soil maps circa 18-something-or-other that graph the geology and topography of our meadow, which used to belong to a much larger farm. I imagine large scrolls painted mostly pale green with blue lines for rivers and streams, and forest-green lines of undulating or concentric coils that look like the whorls of a fingerprint denoting hills and valleys. I imagine the musty smell of dust, mothballs, and cellar.

In contrast, we look at the maps on a large-faced computer. Our soil specialist can  zoom in on our eight acres of land with several clicks of the keyboard. There before us is an aerial photograph of our property taken before we took down the old garage, before we built the new carriage barn, before we moved a stone wall, before we re-roofed the house. The land looks green, except for the well-worn doe-colored path from the house to the garden, and the doe-colored square of our neighbor's recently mowed field.

Our specialist prints out a copy of the map, which smells more of petroleum and wax than dust and mothballs. He also prints out the series descriptions of the soil making up the pieces of our land. We read through them together, and Caleb and I think the description is mostly right, but we know we have areas that do not drain well, where the Sensitive Fern turns yellow and brown in fall, suggesting wetter and more acidic land. Since we have dug garden beds in this earth, we know there is a significant amount of clay, which we think bodes well for grapes, as well as pockets of sand where we know we can grow lavender, and there is an ever-ready supply of rocks and stones continually rising to the surface pushed by some internal movement at the center of the earth.

While our notes are already quite particular, we agree with the soil specialist that we should submit a new sample to get an even more specific look at the makeup of our dirt. Although it is early winter, we know the ground has not yet frozen and that we can successfully dig the ten to twenty samples that we must mix to make a true and accurate composite of the land we want to know better.

The Soil Kit Questionnaire is fairly simple. Question 1: Sample identification or field name? This seems straightforward, but I realize this is a perfect opportunity to name the site like a grand cru vineyard. What should we call it? Gattamora, after the two black cats who live with us in our house? Or Cervo Nero, to honor the mythic black deer that the previous owner told us haunts the field? Of course, we are attracted to the Italian, but maybe we should call it something more historical like Lamb Hill after the two lambs who lived in the potting shed so many years ago.

The other questions on the test are easy: the size of the plot of land to be tested, the soil texture, the drainage, the crop to be planted, and whether this will be commercial or for the home. Question 6—Would you like organic fertilizer information?—strikes me as somewhat similar in tone to the question on the doctor's office questionnaire, "Would you like to discuss sexually transmitted diseases?" I circle number 33 for "grapes" to check the crop for fertilizer information. Natural, I hope.

While I am waiting for the soil analysis, which may come long after this writing is complete, I decide to do some of my own research. What is micaceous schist? What is siliceous limestone? Will any grape want to find a home here?

*Mica:* One of a group of chemically and physically related aluminum silicate minerals, common in igneous and metamorphic rocks. Characteristically splitting into flexible sheets used in insulation and electrical equipment. From *micre,* to flash.

*Aluminum silicate:* Andalusite from Andalusia, Spain. A gemstone called lapis crucifer made from metamorphic carbon, or clay.

*Schist:* Any of various medium-grained to coarse-grained metamorphic rocks composed of laminated, often flaky parallel layers of chiefly mica. French *schist,* from Latin (lapis) *schistos,* fissile (stone), a kind of iron ore. From the Greek *skhistos,* split, or divisable, from *skhisein,* to split. I think of *schizophrenic.*

The mineral composition of each specific schist is often reflected in its name. It's all highly foliated, medium-grained *metamorphic* rock, which means it has been formed by intense pressure and heat.

*Siliceous limestone:* Rock consisting of mainly calcium carbonate, $CaCO_3$, used in the manufacture of lime, carbon dioxide, and cement. A *sedimentary* rock—one formed from consolidated clay sediments—consisting mainly of calcium carbonate, often in the form of the minerals calcite or aragonite, and even sometimes magnesium carbonate in the form of dolomite. It can contain minor amounts of silica, feldspar, pyrite, and clay. The color is usually white, gray, or black. It forms either through accumulation and compaction of fossil shells of other calcium-carbonate-based marine organisms such as coral, or through the chemical precipitation of calcium carbonate out of seawater deposited by the remains of sea animals.

*Calcium,* also called Atomic Number 20, is a white metallic element that burns with a brilliant light. It's the fifth most abundant element in the earth's crust.

*Siliceous:* Sedimentary rocks that contain silica ($SiO_2$) and are commonly formed from silica-secreting organisms such as radiolarians, known more widely as amoeba, protozoa, and zooplankton; also found in diatoms, or phytoplankton, both of which originated during or before the Jurassic period, or the Age of Reptiles. The rocks can also be formed from certain types of sea sponge that produce spicules made of silica calcium carbonate.

*Calcareous rock:* Sedimentary calcium carbonates such as calcite or aragonite.

*Jurassic period:* Named by Alexander Brongiart for

the extensive maritime limestone exposures of the Jura Mountains where Germany, France, and Switzerland meet.

In our kitchen pantry, we have six bottles of *vin jaune,* the idiosyncratic white wine made like a sherry that comes from the French Jura. I wonder if our soil would be habitable to this grape called Savagnin, somehow the same grape as Gewürztraminer from the town of Tramin in northern Italy, also known as Gringet in the Savoie in France—which apparently also has a similar soil composition to ours, with its *micaceous-siliceous* content. They grow Mondeuse and Mondeuse Noir in the Savoie; Mondeuse Noir, a red, is thought to be the same grape as the ancient Refosco grown in the Italian region of Friuli on the Slovenian border. In Friuli, they have calcium-rich marl with *flysh sandstone* made up of clay, gravel, and sand.

I consider naming our plot of land Atomic Number 20, or Lapis, or Skhistos, or Chateauguay, or Feldspar, or the Fifth Element. In Italian, it becomes *Elemento Cinque.* But we think that while we may call our label something Italian, while we may name the individual wines something Italian to honor our joint experience, we feel it is important to name the plot of land something appropriate to our landscape. I fill in the question on the Soil Kit Questionnaire: C15.

− 3 −

*bitter alchemy*

$T$hey say this is a Sicilian recipe: Gather roses in perfect bloom during the hottest hours of a June day when their perfume is at its headiest. They say, pluck the roses and separate the petals from the flower. Trim the white moons from the base of the petals; these will be too bitter, they say ("they" being those who knew, Sicilians recording a family recipe at the end of the nineteenth century).

Steep the rose petals in a grain or fruit alcohol for a fortnight along with a vanilla bean. When the two weeks are up, strain the liqueur and remove the rose petals and vanilla bean. Prepare a simple syrup of sugar melted in water on the stove. Add the simple syrup to the liqueur. Set aside in a dark corner of your pantry for another fortnight. Filter and bottle. Serve after a good meal. The drink will be quite strong, but quite nice, they say.

This is a recipe for *rosolio,* a sweet yet bitter liqueur enjoyed by young ladies and grandmothers in the nineteenth century, and found in *mangia e be' i*—literally translated as "eat 'n' drink"—light beignets filled with *rosolio* and sold at country fairs a hundred, two hundred, three hundred years ago. In Italy, *rosolio* is still enjoyed after a lengthy meal, or late in the afternoon, or before going to bed. This particular recipe was found in the musty pages of an old cookbook in a dark, narrow used-book store in Spaccanapoli, the old center of Naples, where the cookbooks were sandwiched between Italian Victorian erotica and a stand of old postmarked postcards. I wrote the recipe down in a little notebook, then chose two post-cards, yellowed watercolors of towns in Campania with faded spidery ink on the backs (*"sunny and warm, with much love—"*).

As I write this, in Vermont, it is now late August. I pick my roses. I should have been gathering them in July when they were at their fullest and most obscene. I have had difficulty procuring the grain alcohol. I've been trying since July, but my local liquor store does not stock grain alcohol, a 190-proof distillation most widely used in this country for college parties where the hosts mix garbage cans full of fruit juice and Everclear (the trade name of a certain grain alcohol), and the guests drink the cocktail like water. Grain alcohol has very little flavor when mixed with other elements, making it easy going down, easy to forget you're drinking a cocktail, easy to get drunk. If you drink too much, too fast, it can kill you. An adaptation of my recipe tells me I can use vodka if I'm unable to get the grain alcohol, but I've had *limoncello,* another Italian after-dinner cordial, made with vodka and I found the taste to be all wrong, the vodka imparting a distinctive leather note despite its generally clean flavor. Perhaps the vodka was all wrong.

So I wait for my three bottles of grain alcohol to arrive at the local state liquor store, a special order I have had to discuss with the owner. He knows I'm well over twenty-one, and I've explained my plans to him. No garbage-can parties for me. I'm playing at alchemy. I'm making *amaro*. I'm making *rosolio*.

*Amaro*, which means "bitter" in Italian, is a kind of after-dinner cordial, a *digestivo*. Like a short cup of espresso, it settles a good meal. *Amaro* is particular to Italy, and *rosolio* is particular to Sicily and Calabria. Each region in Italy has its own style and recipe, and these *digestivi* can be made from herbs or walnuts, roses or lemons. They have antique, floral-sounding names, which are pronounced with an almost religious fervor: Amaro Lucano, Ramazotti, Vecchio Amaro del Capo, Jannamaro, Padre Peppe.

I go to pick up my order two weeks later, and no one can find my three bottles of grain alcohol in the stockroom. I wonder about the young clerk, about summer parties, and then I place the order again. A few weeks later, my husband picks it up for me, but the young gentleman working, his skin still pocked with high school acne, will only let him take one bottle at a time. Maybe if the manager were here, he could take all three, but the young gentleman doesn't want to take any chances. My husband, who like me is well over twenty-one, gets carded frequently.

So here I am at the end of August, picking the last of my rose blossoms during the hottest point of the day, peeling the petals away from each flower, then trimming those white bitter moons. I'm preparing my concoction on the dining room table that my husband and I made six years ago on Thanksgiving Day before friends arrived to feast. I'm wondering how I got here, at the end of August, picking the last of my roses, as obsessed as a perfumer to pick the most fragrant, most luscious, most velvety of roses—one and three-quarter ounces of them, to be exact. After I have trimmed their pale crescents, I stuff them with a chopstick down the neck of a bottle of grain alcohol.

This bit of alchemist's pleasure comes to me from Italy. When my husband and I first lived there, we were introduced to *vin santo,* holy wine. This is the traditional Tuscan after-dinner drink served with *cantucci,* those little almond biscotti that are dipped into the thick, mead-like wine. From there, we became enamored of grappa, the Italian *eau de vie.* Grappa—a distillation made from grape skins after the fruit has been pressed for winemaking—can be either sublime, smooth, and scented of saddle leather, or quite rough, tasting like lighter fluid. We became collectors of grappa, fascinated and infatuated with the interesting shapes of the bottles and with the out-of-the-way vineyards that took the effort to make them. And from here, we made the leap to *amaro.*

We had always been curious about those brightly labeled bottles we saw on café bar shelves, and aware of the old gentlemen in their tweed jackets and squire's caps standing at the bar. They were holding heavy, elegantly shaped, tall shot glasses full of dark liquid. However, it wasn't until we traveled to the south of Italy that we were introduced to the father of all *amari* in the hauntingly beautiful cave city of Matera.

In the deep heart of Basilicata, the anklebone of Italy, the city of Matera beckons. Once a condemned, impoverished place, once called Italy's shame, Matera is and has always been noble. These days the city has been reenergized with

Materese pride; it is thriving and in a constant state of rebuilding. Our hosts there sent us out on an unusually foggy night to a little place serving some of the best of the local food. It was at the Trattoria Lucana that we became members of the converted.

At Trattoria Lucana, the lights were warm and bright, the tables were full, and the room was noisy. The walls were lined with black-and-white photos from the fifties and earlier, images of Materese sitting in front of their arched cave doorways. These were the non-Christians that Carlo Levi once wrote about in his book *Christ Stopped at Eboli,* the "peasants" whom UNESCO removed from their malarial caves in 1956.

Our waiter Enzo, who, by his features, seemed descended from those proud cave dwellers, was friendly. After a brief conversation with him, we decided to ask him to order for us. Dressed in his white shirt, black bow tie, and red vest, he looked authoritative. He poured us Aglianico, the kingly grape of the south, which is dry, big, elegant, and less than ten American dollars a bottle. Then the food started to arrive.

I must tell you about the food in order to tell you about the *amaro,* because *amaro* almost always follows the food, as the final note to the coda, to the orchestration that is a meal. At least nine dishes of antipasti came to the table. We ate fresh ricotta, and *sformate,* wedges of egg and herb or rice tart. Enzo delivered plates of little fried things: slices of eggplant, zucchini, olives. Then he served us red peppers, the edges of the slices charred black with roasting.

There were *orecchiette,* little handmade ears of pasta, tossed with braised *cima di rapa* and seasoned with hot *peperoncino.* We ate simple roasted meats: lamb, beef, chicken, pork sausage, all of them flavored only with salt, pepper, rosemary, olive oil, and wood smoke. Then the *dolci,* our dessert, which I don't remember exactly, though I do remember the richness of this table. Such evenings have made me understand that Italy's true wealth is in the food of the poor.

Enzo asked if we wanted espresso to finish, or *amaro.* Because we like a good adventure, we chose *amaro,* but there was a further question from Enzo. "Fernet-Branca, or Padre Peppe?"

Fernet-Branca is a ubiquitous national brand. We didn't know Padre Peppe. Our momentary silence as we tried to make a decision was all Enzo needed. "Padre Peppe it is then."

Padre Peppe is made by Franciscan monks in the plains of Altamura, only forty kilometers from Matera, still considered local even though Altamura is technically in another region. The lines between places written on paper become somewhat blurred in this part of the world. Padre Peppe is an elixir of walnuts—so its label says. Ours was hot and sweet and medicinal and went down with ease. We experienced a conversion, a glow of warmth radiating from our windpipes to our stomachs.

*Amaro,* or drinks like *amaro,* have been made for a long time. Their origins within convents and monasteries include the practice of steeping herbs in alcohol, usually wine, as a means of preserving their medicinal properties. Growing seasons could be short and winters long, especially in the many mountainous places to which religious orders had fled to practice their faith undisturbed.

Among some of the earliest writings on the subject of flavored alcohols are those found in the journals of the Catalan Arnold de Vila Nova, an alchemist in Spain and France who was born in 1240. In his *Book of Wine,* he wrote of the distillation of wine into *aqua vitae* and of the flavoring of those spirits with various herbs, fruits, and spices. In particular, he addressed *aqua vitae*'s healing and restorative powers. One of de Vila Nova's students, a certain Raymond Lully, even believed that these flavored *aqua vitae* were so powerful and vital that their crafting was an inspired gift from Heaven.

During the Middle Ages, these distillations were primarily known as alchemical potions and made only by alchemists, especially those belonging to religious orders. It wasn't until a much later date that the "potions" were enjoyed as secular cordials. By the fourteenth century, these drinks had become popular in Italy and France, a popularity often attributed to the court of Catherine de' Medici, the Italian aristo who married into French royalty. It is said she brought the recipes and the use of these liqueurs to France from her native Tuscany. But there is also some evidence of an earlier diffusion of this type of drink, or an independent outgrowth of these distillations prior to their introduction by Catherine. There is no doubt, however, that the Medici court, so focused on food and the pleasures of the table, increased the interest in these *amari* among the nobility of France.

Between the fourteenth and the early seventeenth centuries, monastic orders and village alchemists became the primary producers of *amari*. In the Abbey of Fecamp, around 1510, Don Bernardo Benedictine created the drink called Benedictine. The recipe for Chartreuse was originally called an *Elixir de Longue Vie* (Elixir of Long Life), given to a Carthusian monastery near Paris by the Marechal d'Estrees, a captain under Henry II, husband to Catherine de' Medici. Cusenir Mazarine, a French anise liqueur, dates to a 1637 recipe from the Abbaye de Montbenoit. Recipes, too, for herbal liqueurs like the Pugliese Padre Peppe were also originally monastic in origin. But it would be a mistake to claim that production of liqueurs was limited to monasteries and convents. By the middle of the sixteenth century, several secular distilleries throughout Europe had been formed and were producing commercial quantities of *amari* and cordials. These included the Dutch distillery of Bols, founded in 1575, and Der Lachs, a German distillery that began producing Danzig Goldwasser in 1598. The first liqueur that Bols turned out was made from anise collected wild in the fields.

A commercially prepared and sold *amaro* didn't make its appearance in Italy until the mid- to late 1800s. Fernet-Branca began producing its line of cordials in 1875, Padre Peppe in 1835. Prior to that, *amaro* was a home brew. Fortunately, it still is.

The word *liqueur* comes from the Latin *liquefacere,* to melt or dissolve, and refers to the method used to flavor the whiskies, brandies, and grain alcohols that form the base of any liqueur. And there are several methods of *liquefacere:* maceration, distillation, and percolation. The end result of any of these methods is the same, not unlike the process of making a perfume: the flavor/scent of the fruit, spice, or herb is dissolved into the alcoholic base. The choice of method depends on the properties of the fruit, spice, or herbs, as well as the particular flavor desired in the final liqueur. Some additives will flavor differently, depending on which process is followed.

For the home cook, *maceration* is the most typical process and the simplest. The aromatic flavoring—be it rose petals, lavender, violet, cherries, or strawberries—is bruised, then steeped in the alcohol for a period of time in order that the essence may be extracted. This essence is then added to the final base of the liqueur. *Distillation* refers to the intensification of the desired flavor that has already been macerated. It is a reduction often repeated several times, with a large volume of the flavor becoming a relatively small, stronger amount. This essence is then added to the bulk of the alcoholic base. In *percolation,* either water or alcohol is allowed to drip through the flavor ingredient, or else the ingredient itself is heated, and the steam of the also-heated alcohol or water passes through the flavor before it recondenses.

Simple maceration is just right for a juicy fruit. Liqueurs using citrus do not obtain their flavor from the juice, however, but from the oil in the fruit skins, and this is usually done through percolation. Distillation and percolation are most commonly used for extracting flavors from the tough skins of certain fruits, and also from harder and drier ingredients, such as spices.

By using different methods, different flavors can be extracted from the same source. In many spice-flavored liqueurs, a more bitter or astringent flavor will result if an alcoholic base is used in percolation rather than water. Depending on the taste and the type of liqueur desired, the process and base liquid should be carefully considered.

Once any of these three processes has been used, the remaining steps in production tend to be the same: Mix the final blend of the aromatized base, and, if necessary, set it aside to age. Or mix the blend and add any desired sugar and/or water, to be followed by a generally short period of aging, which will promote the marriage of aromatics to alcohol. Then there is coloration, cold stabilization, and, finally, bottling. In the fourteenth century, our methods of coloration and cold stabilization would not have been considered—or deemed necessary. These are modern inventions for large-scale commercial production. When you make an *amaro* at home, you don't need to worry about altering the color or providing cold stabilization. You leave both to nature and alchemy, and follow in the footsteps of medieval alchemists, or monks, or Baroque royal chefs.

This is what I like about making something that has existed for hundreds of years: I taste history. This is why my husband and I have collected *vin santi, grappe, eaux de vie,* and now, ever since Enzo introduced us to the pleasures and varieties of Italian regional *digestivi, amari.* It is why, when in Italy, my husband and I walk into little wine shops and groceries to ask the *padrona* about the local brew. This is why we follow directions to out-of-the-way *osterie* (country cafés) to eat, then partake of the *rosolio* table, a tasting of five different *rosolii*. These liqueurs, prepared in the kitchen, are made with coffee beans, or violets, or rose petals, or nuts and anise, or a mixture of saffron and spices.

I have the great bonus of a rose garden. Along a stone wall to the south of our Vermont home is a hedge of mixed roses, which grew here long before we bought the property. They were planted, I'm told, by the lady who originally built our house. She had a legendary rose and wildflower garden. The owners who came between her and us destroyed much of her efforts through blind-sightedness and neglect, and I now work hard to resurrect and nurture the few plants that are left. I've tried to classify her roses, looking in gardening books, asking knowledgeable friends. No one really knows what they are, except for a local man whose family has been here since the French and Indian War. He tells me that the pink roses with six petals and the yellow center are "seaside roses" brought to our mountain by a transplant. She transplanted not only herself, but also a part of the place from whence she came, and these roses do give our open field and wide-view landscape a decidedly seaside look. On a moonlit summer night, as my husband and I walk home from the neighbor's house, the wind in the trees sounds a lot like the ocean.

My old lady's roses have inspired me. Many other varieties now bloom in a more formal garden: 'Seafoam', 'Mother's Day', 'Madame de Bourbon', and 'Gene Bruner'. This is the mixture that I use to make my concoction, my *rosolio,* and the Latin captures it: *ros solis,* sun's dew. I've picked at high noon, just as my old recipe says. I've bought a bottle of Graves grain alcohol (another brand from Everclear), and I've trimmed the white moons from the rose petals. I've stuffed the petals down the neck of the bottle, because I didn't have a jar with a big mouth and lid. Now I wait. Two weeks later, I will make my simple syrup, straining out the pale, colorless petals, fragile as moth's wings. I'll remove the vanilla bean, then add the simple syrup and set the jar aside—again to wait.

It is a cold, rainy October day when my husband and I first taste the *rosolio.* The rain falls horizontally, and the National Weather Service has issued a High Wind Alert. We are in the middle of a house renovation; and, because the roof is off, with only our cedar ceiling and a large tarp between us and the elements, leaks have sprouted around the windows and in certain places in the roof. There's no reason this should be happening—the house has been amply protected against the weather—except that the wind is so strong it blows its way behind the window trim and insinuates itself beneath our roof tarp.

As a quick remedy, we have lined the bottoms of the windows and French doors with plastic and newspaper. A few plastic buckets are positioned throughout the house to catch steady drips. We've finished eating a lunch of grilled ham and cheese sandwiches with a leek soup I made from the last of the leeks I pulled from the garden yesterday. Such a plebeian lunch, we decide, needs an elegant finish. We get out our cut-crystal decanter and Georgian sherry glasses—petite, stemmed glasses with fluted bowls that I found in a junk shop north of here. We pour ceremoniously, the color of the *rosolio* a pale, almost tea-stained hue. The scent is intense and alcoholic. I am pleased and surprised that the taste is multilayered—first, the essence of rose, almost like a perfume, then the vanilla, and a sweetness behind that, with a fiery finish. I feel it in my throat and down my windpipe. The recipe did say it would be strong, and the recipe is also right in that it *is* nice. My husband and I discuss possible refinements: Can I cut the fervent alcohol taste? Can I tame it just a little? We decide that tomorrow I will make another simple syrup of half a cup of sugar dissolved in a cup of water and add that to my brew to see if it banks the fire.

That night we dine with some friends. In their dining room on a side table are jars full of *liqueur rouge,* a southern French style of *rosolio* made of brandy, raspberries, red currants, and cherries. They made this batch of liqueur in July when they, in great fortune, found cherries, red currants, and raspberries ripe and available all at the same time. After forty days of maceration, our friends added simple syrup to taste. They've been making *liqueur rouge* for years, after first trying their hand at using an old southern family recipe of peaches steeped in bourbon and sugar, started in July (when peaches are in season in Maryland) to be ready for drinking by Thanksgiving.

After a dinner of Cambodian curry flavored with peanuts, coconut milk, basil, cilantro, mint, and a hot-pepper fish sauce, we taste their *liqueur rouge.* The *digestivo* is red in color, but clear, like cranberry juice, and I taste all three elements of the fruit with the raspberry and currant the strongest. It is slightly sweet, and our host tells me this bottle may have had a cinnamon stick added. We compare recipes and tastes, and talk of an orange liqueur made with a handful of coriander seeds. I wonder whether such a concoction, if I start now, would be ready by Christmas.

This is why I've spent the last four months preparing my *rosolio,* why I carefully cut the white moons off my rose petals before steeping them in pure alcohol: this is part of my philosophy of taste. Taste is connected to history, the history of the table, which is, after all, a narrative history, an oral history. The tongue experiences; the mouth tells a story.

At the table, we share these stories. My husband and I, alone in our leaking house, tasting our *rosolio,* reminisce about the *rosolio* we tasted in the mountains of Calabria. We remember being at our friends' table, talking of the myriad versions of after-dinner liqueurs and imagining how our stashes would get us through the fall and the long, cold Vermont winter. I recall the generosity of hosts in Italy who plied us with their regional, or family, liqueurs. I remember an Easter dinner at the seaside near Rome where we stayed up late and tasted *nocino,* a green walnut liqueur, as well as *limoncello* and a home brew made by the caretaker of our host's Rome apartment building, a brew so potent that it defies explanation. I wrote the recipes on the back of a paper napkin.

Yes, this is why I learned to make this *rosolio:* to quell the Demon Alcohol in my family's history through the scrupulous attentiveness that is needed in performing the magic, the alchemy of capturing my garden in a bottle. This effort creates a *new* experience of alcohol, and it connects, to make two things at once, a recipe and a story, both shared at the table.

〜

### recipe for rosolio

Pick roses at the hottest point of the day—red roses, for they will impart more color and flavor to the alcohol. (If you do not have your own rose garden, I recommend procuring your roses from a friend or a local grower so that you can be certain that the blooms have not been treated with any chemicals.) Separate the petals from the flower. Trim the white edge at the base with a knife or scissors. Weigh out 1¾ ounces petals, then steep the petals in a jar of 190 proof (95 percent) pure grain alcohol with a vanilla bean in a large canning jar. Close the jar and set aside in a dark place for two weeks. After two weeks, strain the liquid, removing the rose petals and vanilla bean. Prepare a simple syrup by dissolving 1 pound sugar and 3¼ cups water. Add the simple syrup to the alcohol, return the mixture to the jar, and store for another two weeks. At the end of those two weeks, filter and bottle. After your first tasting, more simple syrup can be added if desired to cut the hotness of the alcohol and suit your taste.

〜

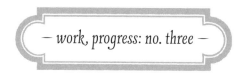

— *work, progress: no. three* —

*In about* AD *1000, the intrepid Scandinavian Leif Eriksson the Lucky crossed the North Atlantic and arrived along the coast of North America. He named his discovery Vinland in honor of all the grapevines he found.*

The Minnesota Grape Growers Association lists nineteen wine grape varieties indigenous to Minnesota. These varietals are hardy down to −20 degrees F. Other grapes there have been developed in other cold-weather climates around the world; they have been accepted into US quarantine programs and will be released in two to three years if all goes well with virus testing. Seven currently available varieties, two red and five white, are being grown in vineyards all around Vermont: Frontenac, Marquette, Frontenac Gris, St. Croix, La Crescent, and both Swenson Red and Louise Swenson. One of the oldest wine vineyards in Vermont, Shelburne Vineyards, has also started to work with the traditional European grapes Riesling and Zweigelt.

In New York State, vineyards grow Riesling, Cayuga, Chardonnay, and Marechal Foch. In Quebec, just a few hours over our border, they grow Seyval and Sabrevois as well. It is logical that we will research any and all of these varieties, taste wines being made by local vineyards, and choose what to plant from this collection of proven standards. We will grow these grapes, and when ready make wine from them. But illogical thoughts creep in. What if we were to also start experimenting with grapes from Italy that we feel would do well in our climate, our soil? After all, grapes thrive in the Italian Alps, where they make beautiful prismatic wines. Why not in the much softer, older Vermont hills?

We begin to think wishfully. The grape Nebbiolo, which makes the wines known as Barolo, Barbaresco, and Sforzato, grows in cold, fog, and at the foothills of alpine mountains. But we know in the end this finicky grape would probably not thrive here. The Austro-Italian varieties seem like possible choices: the Rieslings, Gewürztraminers, Sylvaners of the north. We circle around possible reds. I think of the brambly, wild, and very rare reds of the Val d'Aosta: Fumin, Cornelin, and Prëmetta. I think of the bold, structured red of the Friuli: Refosco, which grows on the Slovenian border. Refosco del Peduncolo Rosso, its full name, translates to "Refosco of the Red Foot" because the vine is actually red at its base. Refosco is the Red Mondeuse in the French Savoie.

While I think forward to experimentation, I also think backward to reinvention. What about Leif Eriksson's numerous vines that grow wild all around us? Why is no one making some kind of wine out of these grapes? Or hasn't made wine in a very long time? (Certainly New England farmers must have made rustic wines along with their ciders to get them through the long winters.) Early civilizations like the Persians, the Etruscans, the Greeks, the Romans all made wine from grapes they found in the countryside. They took what was wild and cultivated them. They flavored with honey those that were unpalatable. The

Greeks and the Romans carried vine stock with them to lands they conquered, spreading their own once-wild varietals all over Europe.

In Europe, the main grape species is *Vitis vinifera.* In northeast America, the main varietals are *V. riparia* or *V. labrusca.* There are about eighteen other clones or subvarieties, but the main vines are these two. Here in Vermont, we call our wild grapes frost grape, or fox grape, or vixen grape. It goes by many other names as well: Michaux, Mignonette Vine, riverbank grape, Bermuda vine, scented grape, Vignes des Battures, Vitis Amara, Le Conte, June grape, and winter grape. The northeastern fox grape is technically classified as *V. labrusca,* from which the Isabella variety has been developed, and the southeastern fox grape is *V. vulpina,* really just an old name or subvariety of *V. riparia.* Muscadine or Scuppernong, also found in the South, gets its own genus classification now as *Muscadinia rotundifolia* because it actually has forty chromosomes, not thirty-eight like other grape varietals. Concord, Catawba, Niagara, and Delaware grapes are all derived from *V. labrusca.*

For fox grape, the specific name *V. vulpina* is Latin for "fox-like; of or belonging to a fox." In folklore, foxes have been particularly attracted to this variety, hence the common name. Frost grape is called such because the grape is too tart, musky, herbaceous, and acidic to be edible until after the weather is cold enough for frost, which concentrates the grapes' natural sugars and brings their flavor to the surface.

While we have always had abundant vines in North America, Columbus brought European rootstock with him to Haiti in 1494, and from there colonists brought these grapevines to mainland North America. Pests and diseases that did not affect our native grapes feasted and attacked these wine grapes, so they did not take hold, but as North American culture grew, so did the cultivation of the land. More European *Vitis vinifera* was brought across the sea to graft onto the hardy native grape stock, and in this way our cultivated varieties of grapes like Concord and Catawba came into being. *V. riparia* and *V. labrusca* are used widely in American grape-breeding programs, giving us the French-American hybrids like Marquette, Seyval, Chambourcin, and Vignoles. Some researchers have noticed that the wild grapes have even cross-pollinated on their own, making natural hybrids.

In 1860, phylloxera, a plant louse that attacks the roots of grapevines, appeared in France, Italy, and other parts of Europe. Within a few years, the disease almost completely destroyed millions of acres of vineyards. In order to resuscitate the European wine industry, vineyard owners overseas grafted *Vitis vinifera* vines onto American *V. riparia* rootstocks because these wild grapes were so hardy they defied such invasive destruction as phylloxera. Now all winemaking grapes grown at a certain altitude (some high-altitude grapes are not affected by phylloxera because the louse can only survive so many feet above sea level) are grafted onto *V. riparia* rootstock both here in the United States and abroad in order to protect the crop.

On hot days, farmers used to weave wide grape leaves into their hats to shade them from the sun, and farm wives used the leaves as flavor in pickling and in meat dishes.

In the wild, the healthiest vines are often found on river-banks, and they were widely used (and still may be) as a swing rope for launching into the water. The grapes themselves were typically used for jams, pies, and jellies as they are considered to be too "foxy" in taste to be good for wine.

*V. vulpina* was most likely the grape used by Thomas Jefferson's winemaker to produce "colonial style" wine for the household. George Washington is said to have also taken notice of this particular species. On July 9, 1783, Washington wrote a letter to the French minister of state saying that he had not considered importing "exotics" for winemaking since grapevines were common here. He, in fact, expected to have more success than those who did import grapes from abroad. "...Accordingly, a year or two before hostilities commenced I selected about two thousand cuttings of a kind which do not ripen with us (in Virginia) 'till repeated frosts in the Autumn meliorate the Grape and deprive the vines of their leaves. It is then, and not before, that the grape (which is never very palatable) can be eaten." Of course, George Washington became distracted by other events in the intervening years, and he never got around to making wine from his frost grapes.

Our own wild grapes are high-climbing or trailing woody vines with fissured bark. The tendrils, which are lemony in flavor, branch opposite one another, and the leaves are simple, prominently lobed and notched. The flowers are extremely fragrant and usually white or green. The fruit is borne in clusters, small with a blue-black bloom. *V. riparia* is clustered more like *V. vinifera*, and *V. vulpina*, as a subtype, has a more loosely clustered aspect like single berries, making them very easy for birds to feast upon. In the wild, these vines thrive in open areas with good sun exposure and adequate soil moisture, such as along riverbanks, forest clearings, fence lines, and roadsides. Cunning, the vine is very adaptable to a variety of soil chemistries. *V. riparia* has been known to withstand temperatures down to –70 degrees F. The foliage is typically resistant to mildew and black rot, and the roots are resistant to phylloxera. The berries, however, can be sensitive to the same mildew and black rot if the vine is exposed to prolonged wet and humid conditions.

I want to grow all of these grapes. I am quickly running out of viable land, and beginning to look over and covet my neighbors' fields. I must be sensible, though, and plant what is established, French-American hybrids like Frontenac Gris and Marquette, especially since I know that our small experiment with the pergola suggests they will do quite well on our site. I will also begin the long process of sending copies of our soil analysis to winemaker friends in Italy who grow Refosco, Gewürztraminer, and Cornelin and hope to import cuttings from their vines to graft onto our hardy *V. riparia* rootstock. I will also take cuttings of our many Frosty Fox grapes (as I've begun to call them), as stock grows readily from cuttings alone. I will cultivate these and let them ripen on the vine until well past first frost, then dry them on straw mats in the loft of our carriage barn just like the age-old tradition practiced in Italy for making sweet wines. I will vinify and age in small old oak bourbon barrels. I will call this very local, wild dessert wine Vixen.

# – 4 –

## ode to campari

*I*'m trying to remember the first time I tasted Campari. What's difficult is isolating the occasion for the sense of that first taste: the setting, the weather, the conversation. There have been so many occasions, places, and circumstances. I'm trying to remember this particular moment because I've only just realized that a Campari and soda, or Campari and orange, or a negroni, that powerful elixir made of equal parts Campari, gin, and sweet vermouth (unless one doesn't like gin—which I don't, so I substitute vodka) have become a kind of personal madeleine, that theory laid out so languorously by Marcel Proust: that a taste could bring to mind a whole catalog of memory, the key to his remembrances of things past.

Campari stitches together a string of my own remembrances that have formed almost half my life. Somewhere along the line I decided that it was important to mark a place, a new place to which I'd traveled, by saluting it with a narrow, cold glass filled with ice and liquid the color of cochineal, cochineal being that strange and luminous red dye made from the wings of ladybugs. My initial experience with Campari clearly set the stage for my own particular era composed of equal parts adventure, romance, melancholy, and inspiration. I want to examine how a taste passing over the tongue conjures a memory, or a series of memories, allowing a person to experience them over and over again through the tip of the tongue, the sides of the mouth, the back of the throat. By most accounts, we can only sense five flavors, which seems to correspond quite elegantly to the inevitable events that mark our lives: sweet, salty, bitter, and sour, and then a fifth flavor, which I feel is somehow synonymous with the category we might label *inexplicable,* made possible by an amino acid and known by the Japanese as *umami.*

So I follow the braid back, the little woven string of all the glasses of Campari I have known, starting from the one I had just last week on the first hot day of our summer, a five o'clock cocktail after a day of gardening, of cutting back dead canes on roses, of weeding a plot of herbs, of building new cedar boxes for raised beds. This cocktail hour is reminiscent of growing up in an age when parents would break at the end of a hot summer day and mix their gin and tonics or Irish whiskies (why did they never have Campari?) and sit on the porch in the shade, or on the patio next to the white-blooming camellias. This is also what *their* parents did, some with the selfsame brand of Irish whisky, others with a glass of cold, pale local beer.

My husband and I sit with our Campari on the porch, and as we drink we look at the garden we've so carefully tended all day, our glasses sweating in our hands, the evening heat sliding by us. We've marked the first day of our summer not by the calendar, but by the first sip of this bitter, slightly medicinal liquor. My husband proffers a notion: Perhaps every Campari is a first Campari, and each time you drink it the taste surprises you (because you are, on each occurrence, in a different state of mind) and marks the experience that much more clearly, while at the same time bringing on a flood of all the past Campari. Perhaps, he warns, I will never rediscover the original experience.

Trained in philosophy, he continues, recalling a discussion of memory theory from his university days. He remembers a warm spring afternoon in the classroom and the professor, her sleeves still buttoned at the wrist despite the heat, explaining the idea that we attach various tags to memories, and later we find a tag and then, we hope, the memory, provided the memory has not lost its tag, or vice versa. We might have tags for Campari such as: Taste, Campari; Scent, Campari; Location, Campari; Certain Temperature of Air with Quality of Light and Time of Year, Campari; and so on and so on. Anytime we raise a glass of it to our lips, we engage our minds, and we are back at that café table or dinner table, or in that city, or out in the countryside, and we have transported ourselves elsewhere in time, even while tagging a new moment.

On a porch in Vermont on an early-summer evening, we could really be anywhere: We could be on a piazza in Casale Monferrato, in northern Piemonte, sitting under a loggia watching everyone else enact their evening rituals. (Some are riding by on their bicycles.) We could be on a seaside terrace overlooking a quiet spring beach in northeastern Sicily. We could be at the corner brasserie across from the École Militaire in Paris—or in the warm bar in Vienna's Hotel Konig Von Ungarn in winter where we sit on a tufted couch and I need those medicinal properties of Campari because I've come down with a stomach flu. Could we even shuttle back to 1842, to a little bar off the Piazza San Carlo in Turin where fourteen-year-old Gaspare Campari expertly mixes his own bitter concoction? It's a recipe for a brilliant red liquid that he's created with a combination of more than sixty herbs, spices, barks, and fruit peels. I imagine he adds a flourish of bubbly water and serves it to the traveling American couple in the corner. She looks slightly ill from the heat of the city, and the man is in need of refreshment.

Gaspare has been working at the Bass Bar for a couple of years (this is long before child labor laws) as an apprentice *maître liquoriste,* master drink maker, the name given to *bariste* and bartenders to encompass the creative elements of their work. This is at the dawn of European cocktails, *aperitivi* and *digestivi* as part of popular, public culture.

As with the history of all alcoholic beverages, bitter drinks concocted from roots and herbs have been around for a very long time in their medicinal guises. It is said that by the seventeenth century, the term *cocktail* had been coined to describe the practice of plucking the family rooster's tail feathers to dab alcoholic bitters on sore tonsils. I've also heard that it referred to an English custom: a cocked tail (cut tail) on a horse indicated mixed blood; a full tail meant a thoroughbred; *cocktail* thus signified a mixture of traits, or elements. In New Orleans, they say *cocktail* comes from *coquetier,* the name of the double-ended eggcup used to measure drinks in the nineteenth century. Monks have been making mixtures to aid the digestion, or to make one generally feel better, since the Middle Ages. But in the 1840s, café culture was just introducing the idea of mixed drinks as part of social life. *Maître liquoristes* took the magic of the apothecary and applied it cleverly to pleasure. *Maître liquoristes*—not mere bartenders—were the creators of such beauties as Cognac, Armagnac, *marc,* and grappa.

Knowing that he was on to something, young Gaspare hit the road and sold his drink throughout Italy. Twenty years later, in his early thirties, he founded his company, Gruppo Campari, in Milan. In those twenty years, France and Italy had become powerful rivals in the production and consumption of *aperitivi. Aperitivo* makers began using on their labels the names of their home cities, like Milan and Turin, when the product began to be distributed throughout the countryside.

In 1862, Gaspare settled in Milan, his second wife's home city, and opened a café in front of Milan's grand, historic cathedral, the Duomo. In Turin, he opened the Café Campari. His youngest son, Davide, worked there for thirty-three years serving the elite of Turin society, like the well-loved King Vittorio Emmanuele and his Prime Minister Cavour.

In the early 1900s, Davide Campari met and fell in love with an opera singer, a certain Lina Cavelieri. Shortly after they met, Lina moved to Nice to perform there for the summer. In order to follow her, Davide decided to enter the export market officially, and it was then that Gruppo Campari started a long history of international distribution. Davide's lengthy affair with Lina is proudly set forth in the company profile as the "love story" element of the history of Campari.

Though Gaspare Campari had been the creator of the family recipe, it was his son who boldly broke new ground in marketing and advertising. His was the very first liquor company to grasp the concept of branding and how it could affect the public's recognition of a drink. As a first step, the drink became known—and was always referred to—as Campari. Davide then sold the family's signature drink to rival bars and cafés, as long as they agreed to display the CAMPARI BITTERS sign prominently in their locations.

As part of this branding effort, Davide began to work with up-and-coming designers and artists, commissioning a series of posters advertising Campari. His only criteria were: that the brand name must be clearly displayed; that artists must use uncomplicated colors; and that the image of the brand should be incorporated naturally into the design. In 1921, the designer Cappiello created one of the most memorable of the advertising posters. His *Folietto* displayed a dancing clown in an orange peel spiral holding a Campari bottle high above his head.

Today, the recipe for Campari is a tightly held secret. No doubt Campari took on a deliberate cachet from this intrigue. Coca-Cola also promotes the secrecy of its recipe, perhaps in imitation of Campari's strategy. The Campari company maintains a Byzantine system wherein the president is the only person in the world who knows the complete list of sixty-eight ingredients and how they are blended together. It is said that one morning each week, the president personally produces the concentrate with the help of eight assistants, each of whom is privy to only one part of the recipe.

As we sit on the porch, my husband and I follow the memory road, sure that we'll stumble across that first Campari on a terrace somewhere. We find we are sitting with friends on the pea-stone patio of a little hotel called the Stella d'Italia on the edge of Lake Lugano on the border of Italy and Switzerland. It is spring, and the plane trees—severely pollarded (the top branches pruned back) in the European fashion—are sprouting their green leaves. The roses trained to the railing that encircles the terrace are starting to bloom, releasing heady scents of their old gallica line. It is evening, and the sun has just slipped behind an alpen peak, leaving us with plenty of soft light but taking with it the net of jewels it had cast on the water. On the adjacent terrace, a woman walks a lanky black cat on a leash. The sound of a duck landing on the lake startles him, and he leaps into one of the plane trees and will not come down. Each of us drinks our Campari and soda, trying to make the cocktail last, because when we finish we must go in to dinner; and, while we are greatly anticipating dinner, it will mean we are that much closer to the end of the meal, and therefore the end of a blissful day.

Then the memory shifts, or dissolves, and we find ourselves suddenly in Rome. It is a warm October evening, my last evening in Italy before returning home to the United States. I will be leaving behind my husband, who is living outside Florence in a town nestled on a curve in the countryside, so that he can continue his apprenticeship with a baker. Perhaps he will be leaving *me* behind when he gets on the train the following morning? We are walking on our last evening together before our brief separation. We are dressed for dinner, which is not until much later, but we are planning to stroll around to the Trevi Fountain because I am superstitious and like the idea of throwing copper coins and making wishes.

We've left the Hotel Suisse via the long, grand staircase from the fourth floor where it keeps its rooms, and we've been greeted by the little black cat who belongs to the patroness and sits on the doorstep on the ground floor in the wide loggia that leads inward to the courtyard. The little black cat likes to ride the elevator up and down with the hotel guests, and sometimes he sits in a red velvet chair next to the parlor palm in the tiny lobby. I wonder a little about this occurrence of black cats.

On a quiet street, near the famous four corners with the four fountains built into the building niches, we step into a narrow bar. It is there that I am convinced we taste our first Campari and soda, along with a grilled ham and cheese sandwich on flat square bread. The evening is still hot in the city, and the cold bitter taste feels good down the throat, a perfect companion to our snack. I remember the frosted glass wall that separated the bar from the public phone and restrooms, and a lovesick *inamorato* pleading on the telephone with his fiancée to take him back. (No, of course he didn't really mean to go dancing with the American girl after all . . .)

The evening light on our porch has shifted, sunk past the horizon line just enough so that we are now in shade.

I consider my husband's description of the memory tag theory, and I decide I like it in conjunction with the idea that every Campari could be a first Campari, because that is romantic. And somehow this idea mixes well with Proust. I find myself leaving the porch for a moment and searching out my 1928 edition of *Swann's Way,* a book I pilfered from the bookcase in the guest room of my parents' house. I know what I'm looking for is on or around page 70. I don't know why I know this, except that my first coming across Proust's famous passage about a piece of cake dipped in tea—it was a passage I had heard about for years before actually reading it—was one of the great moments of my reading life.

What I'm looking for is actually on page 65 of my yellowed and slightly musty copy. It begins:

> And suddenly the memory returns. The taste was that of the little crumb of madeleine which on Sunday mornings . . . when I went to say good day to her in her bedroom, my aunt Leonie used to give me, dipping it first in her own cup of real or of lime-flowered tea . . . But when from a long-distant past nothing subsists, after the people are dead, after the things are broken and scattered . . . the smell and taste of things remain poised a long time, like souls, ready to remind us, waiting and hoping for their moment, amid the ruins of all the rest; and bear unfaltering, in the tiny and almost impalpable drop of their essence, the vast structure of recollection.

In this drop of essence in my glass—cold, slightly medicinal, and the color of cochineal—my own past hovers and reassembles itself. It holds the little black cats, the coins in the fountain, the summers long gone, and first travels. I sip and each memory, in all its full and strange glory, suddenly returns.

◠

### recipe for vodka negroni

This drink is adapted from an hosteria in the little hamlet of Terano Nuovo in the Abruzzo, not far from Pineto, an old-fashioned seaside resort on Italy's Adriatic coast. The *padrone*, a generous soul, treated us to three rounds of negroni, and would have treated us to more if we had felt more stalwart.

This is the sort of drink that can restore one's faith. In any case, its fuchsia sunset color chases away all the darker moods. A traditional negroni is made with gin, but gin does not always agree with me, and the clean elements of vodka complement the bittersweet of the Campari and sweet vermouth very nicely.

- Ice cubes
- 1 healthy ounce vodka
- ½ ounce Campari
- ½ ounce sweet vermouth
- Lemon twist

Fill a cocktail shaker with ice cubes. Add the vodka, Campari, and vermouth. Shake, then strain into a highball glass over more ice cubes. Finish with a twist of lemon.

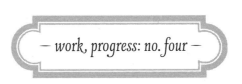

*— work, progress: no. four —*

We are driving along the open expanse of Vermont's Champlain Valley, the broad, open roll of land between Lake Champlain and the Green Mountains. It is a classic summer day: hot, a curtain of haze hanging from the sky to the earth, a soft sun heating the gauze of the air. We drive with the windows open, the scent of dairy farms pungent as we pass them.

We are making a trip to a vineyard that we've recently heard of. We are also making this trip based on nostalgia, stopping in a town we used to live in, exploring roads that used to mark our days, marveling at how much it has changed, how much we've changed, and how much it has all stayed the same. Some changes are discouraging—the development of the small shopping strip in town and the "caught-in-a-time-warp" sameness of some of the shops on the main street; but other changes are exciting—the presence of a Wednesday-morning farmer's market loaded with breads, cheeses, and fruits, and the evolution of a local

strawberry patch we used to frequent as a young 1
couple into a vineyard.

To the outsider, vineyards continue to seem an unlikely
aspect of Vermont life. Our growing season is wistfully
short, and for seven to eight months of the year we are
cold or covered in snow. When people think of wine and
vineyards, they think of the temperate climes of California
and Southern Europe, Australia and South America, or
South Africa.

But this is all in the imagination, I convince myself.
Parts of Italy, France, and Spain are alpine, with plenty
of glacial snow and cold. And they make wine in these
places. At least several other people have thought these
same thoughts in Vermont, for there are several vineyards
here, and more being planted all the time. If New York
State could do it, if Quebec could do it, why not Vermont?

Our local vineyard stories are inspiring. An on-the-
edge-of-collapse dairy farm takes a chance on a fledgling
wine economy and plants eight thousand vines in fields
that used to feed cows. A veterinarian who lives near Lake
Champlain and has a passion for wine and agriculture
plants his plot of land with neat rows of grapes. A strawberry farmer who has a passion for making wine as well
pulls up the small-fruited strawberry vines and replants his
fourteen acres with Frontenac Gris, Frontenac, Marquette,
St. Croix, and Swenson.

Lincoln Peak is the name of this ex-strawberry-patch
vineyard, and it is one of the prettiest I have ever seen.
Perhaps I feel this way because vines planted in this

landscape still seem strange, yet I feel the contours of our meadows and fields lend themselves to grapes, and I want to root for these young vines that are starting to grid the landscape.

The rows are neatly mowed, the vines lush with mid-summer fruit, the roses planted enticingly at each row showing the health of the earth. Between the vines, the grass is kept close-cropped, but there, an earmark of natural winegrowing. The tasting room is built near a pond with cattails edging the water. I remember this building from years ago as more ramshackle and utilitarian when we would come at the beginning of summer to pick berries, eating along the way, our lips and fingers stained with the fresh red fruit.

We taste four of the five wines the vineyard offers, all of which are extremely well made. The dry white, the Frontenac Gris, reminds us of Sauvignon Blanc with its grapefruit character. The semi-dry white calls to mind a Muscat or Moscato d'Asti. The rosé is a balanced blend with berry fruit and an earthiness calling to my mind an obscure Calabrian *rosato* I serve at the restaurant. When we taste the red, we are slightly nervous. I think of this as the truest test of the winemaker in Vermont. We smile. It is dry at the finish, elegant on the palate, and honest in its flavors. The vines are only six years old, just beginning to find their roots in the earth, to feel at home in this new *terroir*. In the future, they will mature in flavor, adding even more depth to their character.

# – 5 –
# *from thorns, grapes*

The poet gathers fruit from every tree,
Yea, grapes from thorns, and figs from
Thistles, he.

Sir William Watson

*C*oenobium. A closed cell structure, like a honeycomb. A religious order closed to the outside world with one single authority, like a convent or monastery. Coenobium is the name of a wine we drink that has traveled thousands of miles over an ocean to find its way into our restaurant and onto our table.

Coenobium is made by Cistercian nuns. For ease we refer to it as the Nuns' Wine. The label is handmade in that classic, looping European script. The wine is organic, and the label is made from recycled paper. The wine itself—when we first tasted it a vintage ago—is pale yellow, crisp like the juice from a lemon. On the palate it is rather spicy, like mustard greens. I pair it with dishes made with wild arugula or chicory, pepper matching pepper. It is intriguing, unusual, and unlike anything else I've ever tasted.

In April, Caleb and I experience what we call the "fifth season" in Vermont, or Mud Season, which is usually drab and wet with rain and snow. In this time of stasis, we make our annual exodus and find our way back to Italy, reversing the trip of the Nuns' Wine. We leave behind in Vermont the movements not visible to the eye—the ground thawing, the sap in the trees flowing thick from the maples for sugaring. We leave behind those hard little buds on the naked branches that give the hills a reddish haze. Business at our restaurant is quiet enough during this time that we can close up the kitchen. We have put the wineglasses, silver, and plates into the large wooden cabinet that looks as if it were sent on a ship from Sicily (instead of a ship from India). We have paid the rent for the month and locked the doors.

We land in Rome or Milan or Florence or Brindisi—it hardly matters. We are back in Italy, where we are called to the alchemy of recipes and wine. For the past fifteen years—what feels like a lifetime—we have been returning. During these last two years, we have driven an old Roman road, the Via Cassia, which has made us understand that all roads really do lead to Rome. But today we are driving *away* from the ancient city with its characteristic umbrella pines, or *pini marittimi,* its Roman red houses, and shiny streetside cafés. We are driving to a small town surrounded by Etruscan tombs that sits on a hill encircled by thick stone ramparts. The landscape is pastoral, almost like the English countryside, with its verdant fields and weeping willows, roadside thickets, and chestnut and hazelnut groves. There are only a few instances of the tropicality we think of as Italian—the occasional palm tree, and several oases of bamboo that line a stream or marshland.

Once settled into our rented apartment, we are as much in love with Italy as ever. We can see through our window two cows in a meadow, separated by a barely visible fence. Their backdrop reminds us of a painting by Corot: thick trees climbing up a hillside, a partly obscured turret belonging to a crumbled ruin.

This village where we've set up house is conveniently near the place where the nuns make the wine, outside the town of Vitorchiano. A forty-minute drive at most we figure when we look at the red and blue veins on the map. I have asked the importer how and whom to contact at the convent, and I feel a little unsure about the proper etiquette when corresponding with ladies who have taken up religious orders. I grew up Catholic, but it was in the time of Vatican II, when all the formality was stripped from the American Catholic Church. Mass was no longer said in Latin, the communion host was made from a bland, whole wheat recipe rather than the wafer-thin *ostia* that simply melts on the tongue and tastes a little like Chinese crackers. Nuns no longer wore starched wimples and heavy serge habits. They wore lay clothes and could be mistaken for anybody else. I don't remember having much contact with nuns in any case. There must have been a shortage in the southern Indiana town where I grew up. I only remember the strong women who ran the hospital for which my father worked, the sisters of St. Vincent de Paul, who still wore polyester religious habits modernized for the ease of care and movement. I always wondered about this: Should nuns or anyone "of the cloth" be made to feel "easy"? Wasn't the point of religious orders to choose a life of renunciation and difficulty? Or was this idea born of some fascination of mine held over from my days of reading medieval history in college, of my being immersed in the struggles of St. Joan of Arc, Catherine de' Medici, and the French Huguenots? Was I still hooked on my admiration for defiant heroines burned at the stake?

The importer has told us the name of the nun who oversees the making of the wine, the person we should try to see. Caleb makes the arrangements with one of the sisters on the phone. Sister Fabiola is not available when we call, but the nun with whom we speak arranges for us to visit, and asks if we would like to stay for lunch. Lunch with nuns? How could we not accept?

We travel to the convent with a friend, who is the daughter of friends, and we joke about leaving her at the monastery with the nuns. She has never had much interaction with religion, except for a brief stint at Sunday school when her mother decided that she and her three brothers needed to understand something of God and the Bible. Our young friend, at twenty-one, is a bit nervous about meeting nuns, and cloistered nuns at that. None of us are quite sure what *cloistered* means, and Caleb and she look to me (the only Catholic) for answers. Lapsed though I may be, I struggle to explain, and then realize I am as perplexed as they are.

The day is breathtaking, the sky a pure blue and the sun warm and beneficent. The soft air smells of newly mown hay and flowers. We arrive at the convent, which is on the edge of town in a broad plain closer to Orvieto in Umbria than to Rome. The fields are planted with wheat, and the first growth sways slightly in the wind. The buildings are fairly new by Italian standards (one hundred or so years old) and very trim and well kept. The walls, of a soft doe-colored stone, are clad with purple-blooming wisteria. An enormous larch shades the outer courtyard. A well has an intricate gargoyled spigot, the face of a dragon, or horse, or monster.

Our meeting is for ten in the morning, but we are not entirely sure of where to go. A nun is in a little shop with a sliding glass window on the outer courtyard, and we ask her where to find our meeting place. She recommends us to the *portiera* (gatekeeper).

We are led into a small chamber, modernly appointed, where we sit on one side, and the other half of the room is held separate by a beautiful wrought-iron grille. The *portiera* asks if we'd like coffee, and, still sleepy from our early-morning drive, we nod enthusiastically. We wait for several minutes, then the *portiera*, smiling radiantly, brings a tray into her half of the chamber and opens a door in the grille to hand us the tray with three pretty china demitasse cups, a silver coffeepot, and a small bowl of sugar with a spoon. We feel a little bit as if we've come to visit someone in a really nice jail. Our own medieval cloister fantasies of living in a simple yet beautiful building, growing one's own food, cooking, washing, praying, living a completely sustained and enclosed existence, have been rather appealing.

Shortly, Sisters Adriana and Maria Grazia arrive on the other side of the grille. One is young (or I like to think young, for she looks about the same age as I am, somewhere in her early forties); the other is much older. They smile beatifically—a cliché but true. Their faces, which surely saw much of other kinds of living before they joined the Cistercians, are without any traces of stress or anxiety. Their skin is smooth, blemish-free, as if their inner beauty really does shine through to the surface.

We talk of our long journey from tasting their wine at home to making the pilgrimage to their vineyard. We tell them we feel honored to serve their wine to guests at our restaurant. The sisters are stunned to meet people who serve their wine so far away. They have a very small production that serves their needs, plus enough for their local community and a small export. Even so, friends of ours who have a restaurant in the village where we are staying do not know of the Cistercian wine and have never tasted it.

"Do your guests at the restaurant like the wine?" the sisters ask.

"Yes, they do. They love how special it is," I tell them. They smile sheepishly at us and each other, dipping their heads, lowering their eyes, clearly fighting the impulse toward pride.

We talk of their wine consultant, a young winemaker from across the border in Umbria. We ask how he came to guide them in the process. The sisters tell us that Giampiero has a family friend who belongs to the community here in Vitorchiano, and it is through her that he first came to the convent for his own pilgrimage and respite. The convent has a small guesthouse on the premises where a person, male or female, can come to rest from the rigors of their world, to be in silence.

During Giampiero's visits here, he became interested in the wine produced in the cloister. Through him, they found the importer Rosenthal Wine Merchants all the way across the Atlantic in New York City (also Giampiero's importer). The proceeds from the cloister's sales help sustain the community and also benefit the local church. Giampiero acts loosely as their consultant, coming to check the grapes once or twice through the season, and helping them determine the best time to harvest. The nuns, as would be expected, practice as little human intervention as possible. If the natural world is divine, what help does it need from us?

We ask if it's possible to see the *cantina* and the vineyards themselves. The two sisters look at each other briefly, a silent communication between them. "The *cantina* is within the cloister walls," Sister Maria Grazia begins. "And those who are not part of the order are not allowed inside. It is private. But we are quiet here today." She pauses and looks at Sister Adriana. "And you have come all this way ..."

Sister Adriana picks up where Sister Maria has left off. "You may meet us back behind the cloister where there is a gate. You drive out of the courtyard to the left, and turn left again down a dirt road. At the gate, we will meet, and let you in."

In our turn, we are stunned. We hadn't thought the vineyards might be inside the cloister and off-limits to us. Of course, the fact makes sense to us now, and we feel amazed that they are breaking their own rules for us. We realize that we know so little of what is appropriate here; we feel we are in foreign territory without a guidebook.

When we cross the threshold of the gate, we all feel a religious exhilaration of sorts. Perhaps *spiritual* is a better word. We talk of this later, how we felt as if we had entered hallowed ground. The great outdoors is like a cathedral, the sky the cerulean blue of a Tiepolo ceiling, the walls pillared by the fruit trees in the orchard, and tall umbrella pines near the convent buildings. Everything seems the distillation of *good*. A purity pervades the air.

The *cantina* and vineyards are small and beautifully kept. The cement floor in the small bricked building is spotless, and the sisters show us the new fermentation vats, the bottling contraption, and the room where they package the wine to be sent overseas. This year's vintage is still sitting in tanks, and they will bottle it at the end of the summer. We will receive the new wine in Vermont some-time in October. A still life of large demijohns in their straw baskets, sitting on the floor near the entrance and dappled both by the light outside and the shade indoors, makes us feel as if we have walked into a painting by a master.

These two sisters caretake the vineyard throughout the season. They prune and tend the three varieties of grapes: the Trebbiano, the Malvasia, and the Greco. They keep the rows between the vines neat, though they practice the old ways of allowing some weeds to remain and create balance in the soil. At the *vendemmia* (harvest), all the cloister's inhabitants come together to pick the grapes, macerate, and make the wine. A local traveling man with a large press comes for three days while everyone picks and presses and pours into stainless-steel vats. This is not unusual. With so many small producers in the area, the man does a good business in autumn, renting out himself and his equipment. I can imagine the *cantina* at that time, lively with activity, the women in their habits going back and forth like bees during pollination.

I ask if I can take photographs of the *cantina* and vines. I am hoping to take a picture of the sisters, something candid that will catch them at ease, but even before I ask I sense this may be forbidden—just as some indigenous peoples believe that if you take a photograph of them, you steal their souls.

"Yes, you can take photographs," Sister Maria Grazia says, followed by Sister Adriana's "Just not of us." They giggle and twitter like schoolgirls. This refusal seems to be spoken more out of modesty than taboo, but I don't want to make anyone feel uncomfortable or be disrespectful, so I refrain from coaxing and snap pictures instead of the lush countryside and the painterly *cantina*. When another nun drives by on a green John Deere tractor, dressed in the royal blue habit seen on the label of Blue Nun wine, I am sorely tempted, the camera itching in my hand. But I know I am fortunate to be in a place so carefully circumscribed and protected, and I cannot allow myself to become an unwelcome intrusion from the outside world. My desire to take the photograph is like the dirty industrialization of the world outside these walls, the world of questionable commerce and usury, belching machines and hedonism, gratuitous pop culture and instant gratification. I flee "temptation"—and put the Devil behind me by putting my camera in my bag.

We walk through the vines and the orchard. We look at the view. Mountains loom grandly in the distance. "Is that the Gran Sasso?" I ask.

The sisters do not know, and say something to the effect that, to them, they are just pretty mountains in the distance. Yet I glimpse a flicker of knowledge that passes quickly like a match going out, as if they both used to know at one time which mountain and which mountain range framed their view.

In the course of conversation, we come to understand that Sister Maria Grazia had a very successful career in the city—though which city we are not told—before joining the Cistercians, and that Sister Adriana came to the church much earlier in her life, but both women had lived in our world before retreating into this one, and we realize that, when they made their vows here, they let go of materiality and their secular pasts. It is not important for them to know what goes on outside these walls, whether that is Gran Sasso or the Sabine Mountains. That kind of knowledge is irrelevant here. My interest in wanting to know the names of mountains somehow feels unseemly.

The bells begin to ring in the campanile of the church. The sisters start a little as if they are Cinderellas and the clock has struck midnight. At any moment could their carriage turn into a pumpkin? These are the bells for church, they say. We are welcome to join the service if we'd like. Then in half an hour there will be lunch. I think it is perhaps too much to ask my companions to sit through a Mass, so we glance at each other then politely decline. As we get into the car, this seems an abrupt finish to our morning, and the sisters seem to be saying a rather final good-bye.

I ask, "*Ma, ci vediamo a pranzo, si?* We will see you at lunch, yes?"

"No," they say in unison. "You will have lunch at the guesthouse. It is prohibited for you to eat with us in the cloister." They look away, as if regretting this rule at the same time they enforce it.

Of course we cannot eat with them in the cloister. What were we thinking? So we make final farewells and thank them for their genuine hospitality. We feel our own regret in leaving them, and, as we drive out the gate waving and the gate closes behind us, we cannot help but feel like Adam and Eve expelled from Eden.

The lunch table at the guesthouse has been set. The dining room is simple, and only two tables will be occupied. A French priest and a woman sit down together. I decide immediately that I don't like him. He appears pompous, not a man of humility. He reminds me of the priest in the film *Chocolat*. The woman he is with leans in to him earnestly. He does not match her interest in the conversation. They speak in low tones in French. I think perhaps she might be a bit in love with him, and I am sorry for her. They sit with a man who is from Ireland. He speaks in a mixture of Italian and English. He wants to know the meaning of *pranzo*. His table companions do not answer him, but we do from the next table. It means "lunch." The woman speaking French smiles at us. The French priest looks ahead or at his plate as if we do not exist.

Another woman comes to sit at our table. She is attractive and well dressed and has braces on her teeth. We learn she is from Rome and her aunt, who was a sister here, died recently. She had always come to visit her aunt, and had gotten into the habit so much so that she still wants to come for reflection and to remember her mother's sister. She and the French woman have met before while staying at the convent, and they exchange pleasantries. The priest looks ahead or at his plate.

One of the nuns has prepared a buffet for us. First there is soup, a clear broth with *pastine,* or tiny shapes of pasta like what children eat. Then there is pasta, a version of *Cacio e Pepe,* the Roman dish made with a sharp, hard cheese and lots of freshly ground black pepper. There is fish, a white fish simply baked with olive oil and garlic. A bowl of greens, to be dressed with olive oil and vinegar; a basket of bread. About half an hour into the meal, the young nun brings in a big pot of espresso still gurgling from the stove and invites us to have coffee and biscotti when we are ready.

All the while, there is a bottle of wine on each table. It is in unmarked glass bottles, the cork just stoppering the neck. No one else is drinking the wine, and we figure this must be last year's vintage, which we have not yet received at home. We pour a little into each of our short glasses. We offer some to our table companion, but she declines. The color is like golden straw or a golden apple. The nose is faintly of apples as well, something like the roses in my garden that smell of apples and spice. The taste is almost like a smooth cider, pungent and tart. We pour a little more, and eat a little more, and talk a little more, and before we know it the bottle is almost empty, and we laugh and say we might as well finish it among the three of us. I wonder if this is the same wine that they use inside the church, the wine used to symbolize transubstantiation, that Catholic belief that the bread and wine taken at communion become the body and blood of Christ.

After we help clean the dishes, we talk with the young nun and the woman who speaks French (and we come to find out she speaks Italian as well as French) as we sit outside taking in the sun. Our friend asks innocently, "What is it that the nuns actually do here?"

They are not nuns who work in orphanages or teach in schools or nurse in hospital. They remove themselves from the world at large. I am hard-pressed to give her an answer.

Above the door that houses the shop, I have seen written that the cloister was founded on the idea that those who entered would pray for all of us. I try to explain to our friend that these women have chosen a life of meditation because they believe their good thoughts and prayers on our behalf will have an effect in the world. I mumble something about purity of action, and purity of thought, and pure energy floating out about in the cosmos, yet my words trail off, seeming insufficient. For a moment, the reclusion of their lives seems rather selfish.

It is not until I am home and sitting in the potting shed before my own garden on the mistiest and rainiest of days that I think back to our visit with Sisters Adriana and

Maria Grazia, and our friend's question about what they do, what effect the nuns' secluded life has on the world. The apples are heavy on the trees, making elaborate arches of the branches. The roses have started to bloom a second time and the rudbeckia, or black-eyed Susan, inserts itself throughout the garden beds. Thunder rumbles in the distance, and a veil of fog heavily approaches. The stream skirting our property rushes, and a Dangerous Storm Warning has blared on the radio. A breeze is picking up, and a sparrow lands on the garden fence. It is early August, yet we've already had a wood fire in the house, and the crickets sing in the meadow. Caleb is hammering together pieces of old cedar left over from our defunct garage to make long wine-tasting tables. Our own young vines are curling up the wooden stakes that will support them. I imagine I can hear the movement of their growing, like a noisy version of a time-lapse photograph. I am without words, yet surrounded by all this sound.

The answer is clear to me now, so many thousands of miles away. The nuns make wine. They make an elixir that is the manifestation of what nature has to offer them that year. The wine feeds them, the people in their village, and it comes to us so very far away and feeds us. It entices us, intrigues us, makes us thankful, makes us think, makes us remember. This is what the nuns have done; they have made an ancient tradition relevant. Their relationship with the young winemaker has in turn affected the way he also makes wine. They have inspired pilgrimage. In turn, the honesty of their wine that I serve in the restaurant affects the way I want to taste wine, explain wine, and make wine. They have sharpened our senses, increased our appreciation of the cycles of nature. They have proven there is goodness in the world, and in that goodness one can understand the meaning of the divine.

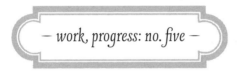

— *work, progress: no. five* —

We have driven home with black plastic crates of grafted vines from Lincoln Peak. We've also ordered grapes from the local nursery, which sit in a row on the front porch in their black plastic growing pots, giving us forty vines in all to plant. Our experimental vineyard, we call it. So we start with four proven varietals: Frontenac Gris, Frontenac, St. Croix, and Marquette. Frontenac was introduced in 1995. It is the first in a series of new varietals developed by the University of Minnesota for northern conditions. A cross of *Vitis riparia* with the French hybrid Landot 4511, Frontenac exhibits many of the best characteristics of both parents. Frontenac is very cold-hardy, tested down to −30 degrees F. The varietal is also very disease-resistant, especially to powdery mildew. The initial acids are high, but often drop dramatically later in the season, and when grown in substantially colder climates the fruit must be left on the vine to mature fully.

Marquette is a cousin of Frontenac and a grandson of Pinot Noir. Marquette was discovered in 1997 in Vineyard Block 1 Row 20 at the University of Minnesota's

Horticultural Research Center near Excelsior, Minnesota. Marquette originated from a cross made in 1989 between MN 1094 and the French hybrid cultivar Ravat 262. Viticulturally, it is outstanding. Resistance to downy mildew, powdery mildew, and black rot have been very good, and its open and orderly growth habit make for easy vine canopy management. Marquette's high sugar and moderate acidity make it a good wine grape. Finished wines are currently showing complex aromas of cherry, berries, black pepper, and spice on the nose and palate. It exhibits a pretty ruby color with pronounced tannins. And all this from vines still quite young.

St. Croix is a blowsier, easier grape, the fun-loving cousin who comes for summer vacation. It is proven cold-hardy to −32 degrees F, and is very resistant to the mildews and black rot. It has a high sugar content and ripens early. It is *vinifera*-like, but with low tannins. It has good fruit, and shows best as a good blending grape, or for making a dessert-style wine. It reminds me of a typical local grape variety called Cagnina in the Emilia-Romagna region of Italy. It is often slightly off-dry with a lovely soft berry fruit, and a sweetness that evaporates easily off the tongue. I serve it at the restaurant with chocolate or simple cakes. It would pair beautifully with a pasta made with fresh ricotta, cinnamon, and a sprinkle of sugar for a hint of sweetness, or a pasta with a sauce made from winter squash, raisins, and pine nuts.

Frontenac Gris is a white grape that was found as a *sport,* or offshoot, of Frontenac, its only difference being that the berries are small, gray, and formed in loose clusters. Frontenac Gris seems to be most suitable for making dessert wines and off-dry table wine, and possibly a very good candidate for ice wine. The grapes ripen midseason with aromas akin to a Muscat: peach, apricot, citrus, and pineapple.

The other grapes we've already planted around the house in seasons past are also Frontenac Gris; we've been tasting several examples of wines produced here in Vermont and have been very encouraged by the results. This grape in particular exhibits a range of flavors and directions—that grapefruity Sauvignon Blanc profile, and a sweet Sauternes note. I can imagine pairing the wine with chicken liver pâté made with orange and dried cherries, or with an orange and radicchio salad, or with an omelet filled with local goat cheese and seasoned with lemon.

We've tilled and prepared the ground for our vines. Caleb digs the holes and I nestle the roots and fill in with our clayey, silty, calcareous soil. We water, we mulch. We talk to the vines, reminding them that they all can make a great wine.

# −6−

## most noteworthy secrets, or alkermes

I

*I* am a young woman, recently wed, living in a small Italian town south of the city of Florence. This is many years ago. I have never been to Europe before, and instead of taking a reconnaissance trip to see how I like it, I dive headlong into a foreign life in a foreign place. I trust my new husband who has been here before me and long talked of the seductions of the red earth, the looming cypress, and the topaz-colored stone houses in olive groves. But even more often, he spoke of a perfect little coffee with a layer of foam as thick as cream, and the most elegant meal he had ever tasted, which happened to be a pizza.

We arrive at the end of September when the sun is still hot and roses still in bloom. The *vendemmia* has begun all around us, but we are too naïve to know that there are people in the vineyards harvesting and crushing grapes. We are too busy trying to figure out where we will live, when the heat will be turned on, and how we will make a living. The first words I learn in Italian are *Posso attaccare questo manifesto per i corsi d'Inglese?* May I hang this poster for English classes? (These words are so embedded in me, they have become like a rhythmic mantra that I might say when I am upset and need to calm myself down.)

The next words I learn are *Una birra rossa o una birra bionda?* A red beer, or a blond beer? These words I say standing behind our friend Gianfranco's newly opened piano bar, the physical waist-high bar I am not allowed to leave during open hours for Gianfranco's fear that I will be harassed by the young wolves come to prey on the new American woman in town. Even though I am married. Such niceties as marriage don't always matter.

Eventually my husband and I are settled in our first apartment tucked into the stone wall of our adopted town, where the heat is still not turned on, the hot-water heater holds only five gallons, and we dry our freshly laundered clothes under a sheet-made tent suspended by two chairs over a space heater in our bedroom. We somehow settle into the pace of our work, teaching English classes and giving dancing lessons, pulling beers and mixing cocktails at Gianfranco's Velvet Underground. We begin to make forays out into our new surroundings.

Every week we buy a train ticket—*andato-e-ritorno* (to go and come back)—and take the train from Castiglion Fiorentino into the city of Florence. An hour and fifteen minutes door-to-door. Arezzo, Montevarchi, Figline Valdarno, Santa Maria Novella—these stops along the way are like Hansel and Gretel's bread crumbs in the forest. Retracing them, we find our way back home. At the station in Florence, a low-slung 1950s building that still holds a shabby but retro cachet, we disembark to the sound of the tick-tick-ticketing of the arrivals and departures boards. I always prefer being *in arrivo.*

Streets fan out from the station like the fingers on a lady's fine leather glove, and one of them becomes our well-trammeled path and entry into the city, Via delle Belle Donne (the Street of the Beautiful Women). A small hotel looks over the worn cobblestones, and several old apartment buildings line a street that is just a little wider than an alley. Laundry hangs out on the balconies, even in the damp fall air that signifies the end of autumn and the beginning of winter. The name of the street is curious, and we wonder if this has always been a slightly seedy part of town. Was this road ever lined with women selling themselves for a few Florentine lire?

Always when we arrive, we follow the same ritual. We walk down the Via delle Belle Donne until it ends at a small coffeehouse that serves the best cappuccino and espresso within shouting distance of the Duomo. The walls are a minty light blue, and there are small round tables with bentwood chairs. The glass pastry case is always full of sandwiches and flaky pastries stuffed with marmalades or cream. The owner is a would-be artist, a mature man with a constant five o'clock shadow and coal-black eyes. Numerous drawings in charcoal on parchment hang on the walls, all nudes. I am still young enough and bourgeois enough to be slightly uncomfortable amid so many lira-size nipples and reclining odalisques. The *caffé* is always packed with students who smoke tarry cigarettes. Mixed in with all the European elegance is a scruffy bohemian-ism that is intriguing and exotic.

Around the corner from the *caffé* sits a simple church decorated in the black-and-white-stone-striped pattern typical of Renaissance Italy. There is nothing fussed-up about the facade—it is actually quite plain—but the square over which it presides is too small for its size, so the church looms, and I get dizzy when I look up to the top framed against the sky. There isn't much to recommend this church other than it is old, and rather fine inside, and was once called Santa Maria della Vigne (St. Mary of the Vines) but is now called Santa Maria Novella, staunchly anchoring one *quartiere* of Florence. Attached to the church, at number 16 Via della Scala, is a little shop, the neighborhood's hidden gem: an apothecary.

This is one of the world's oldest operating pharmacies, the Officina Profumo-Farmaceutica di Santa Maria Novella. It looks as if all the decoration meant for the church has been unleashed in these rooms. Faded frescoes, Baroque furnishings, sparkling glass jars full of powders and pearls of oil, and ancient implements of the apothecary's trade delightfully crowd the spaces. The scents are as glittering as the interior. Bowls full of various mixtures of dried herbs and flowers collected from the hills surrounding Florence perfume the air. The pungent fragrance mingles with the slightly spicy scent of earth, the result of lengthy curing in old terra-cotta jars, their clay coming from the red ground on which this city stands. The scent of this little shop is the essence of the Florentine *terroir*. One knows this instinctively upon entering—though at this time I am too green to know anything more of *terroir* than the definition in my French study books, long abandoned in an attic closet in my parents' home.

Shelves and bottles line the walls of the shop, bottles of perfume called Acqua di Colonia (Water of Cologne), Aceto dei Sette Ladri (Vinegar of the Seven Thieves), Acqua di Santa Maria Novella, and Acqua di Rose. It is said the Acqua di Colonia traveled to Paris in 1500 with Catherine de' Medici, Henry II's blushing fourteen-year-old bride. Old musty history books indicate that she also took along a young scent maker named Renato Bianco who worked for the Officina as her personal *parfumeur,* and that he was as gifted at creating poisons as perfumes. He was the first *parfumeur* to be protected and exalted by a sovereign. His laboratory in Paris had a secret passageway connecting his atelier to her rooms in the palace, where he became known as Rene Le Florentin. After he had made her signature scent (the French called it Eau de la Reine, Queen's Water), Rene Le Florentin set up his own boutique on the Pont au Change. A couple of hundred years later, the Italian Giovanni Paolo Feminis took the recipe for Eau de la Reine to the German city of Cologne and renamed it Acqua di Colonia. It found its way back to Florence under this name.

This library of aromatic waters intrigues, and all of them boast evocative stories like the queen's perfume. The Vinegar of the Seven Thieves dates back to 1600 and it is apparently very useful as smelling salts to revive someone after a fainting spell. Tales tell that the potion was created by a band of grave robbers during the time of the Plague. The perfume supposedly protected them from contracting the disease while they were pilfering the dead. It is said that to safeguard the recipe and their loyalty to one another, each thief knew only one of the ingredients, and the seven would have to come together to create their brew. Not unlike the protocol followed for the current secret recipe for the classic red aperitif Campari.

The eponymous Acqua di Santa Maria Novella has a sedative and antispasmodic effect. Acqua di Rose, in its cerulean blue bottle, has been used since the 1400s as a refreshing tonic for tired and red eyes.

Sitting among all these vials of tonics and scents are a handful of liqueurs: the Elisir di China, made from exotic Asian herbs; the Liquore Mediceo, made in honor of the grand Florentine Medici family; and the Elisir di Edimburgo, an excellent concoction of bitters. A brightly colored, square-shaped bottle nestles between all this glass: alkermes, which sounds like a whisper, an unabashed scarlet alcohol with a label written in a fanciful script. A tag tells me that it was most popular with matrons and young ladies in the nineteenth century, not unlike rosolio, and that the ingredients include sugar, cinnamon, cloves, nutmeg, coriander, and vanilla. Now it is mostly used for pastry, or mixed with mascarpone and sugar for a quick Tuscan dessert. One might think this liqueur colored with Red Dye No. 9. The principal ingredient of alkermes, however, is more poetic. *Kermes vermilio*, long considered by Renaissance Europeans as the perfect red dye, is made from various scale bugs related to the cochineal insect, or from the ruby-colored wings of the ladybug.

This is my first introduction to the mystery of liqueurs. My fingers touch the labels on the bottles of the shelf as if I am trying to divine which elixir will suit me, and my hand hovers over the crimson bottle, then moves on to the blue bottle of Acqua di Rose, which I actually purchase this day and still own, keeping it locked up in my medicine cabinet at home. Yet it is the unchosen bottle of alkermes that

begins to weave a vermillion thread through my burgeoning interest in food and wine.

## II

Years later, alkermes would come back to haunt me. Caleb
and I had returned to Vermont, a place familiar to us both,
and had opened a bakery-cum-restaurant in the Italian
style that had so shaped our early years together. We had
begun a series of return trips to Italy to research old recipes, the ones still cooked in home kitchens, and to trace
their peregrination. We would collect recipes while away
and bring them home to create menus that we honed like
little jewels, but that also had a dose of improvisation. We
cooked what was available and fresh at market, and culled
from our own library of recipes to follow the season and
what grew well near us. We had learned in Italy that it is
assumed the ingredients with which you cook are of your
own landscape. We did not know any differently.

I had become enamored of Italian medieval cooking, an
interest spurred by a gift from a friend of a collection of
French and Italian medieval recipes. This book, and the
story of one of the first great cooks, a man named Maestro
Martino, drove me to the *biblioteca* in Milan to follow my
own research. The recipes I found there also appealed
to the writerly side of me, dishes called Cerulean Blue
Summer Sauce made with blueberries, blackberries, and
ginger, or Goat Roasted in Gold. The recipes sound like
poems, luxuriant and simple at the same time.

In my medieval cookbook, the authors had written a brief section on the medieval cook's use and interest in color. The authors referred to these cooks as alchemists, yet their gold was color rather than metal. Alkanet makes an appearance, as it was known to make the most incredible crimson color. *Alkanet* is another name for our alkermes. I follow the lead of my crimson liqueur, and it takes me back to Santa Maria Novella, where it is said to have been first created by the Dominican monks there. But in actuality, the recipe for the liqueur probably came to Tuscany via Spain and is mostly likely Arabian in origin. *Kermes* means "red insect" in Persian, and in the Middle East a relative of cochineal can be found on a species of oak, called the kermes oak. The insects contain coloring analogous to carmine. *Alquermes* in Spanish comes from the Arabic *quirmiz,* scarlet.

In 1523 in the New World, Hernán Cortés heard about the existence of *nochetzli,* or *grana,* a red dye used by the Aztec and Mexican Indians. Specimens of *grana* were taken back to Spain shortly thereafter, and cloth merchants as far north as Antwerp began buying the powdered dye by the 1540s. Early alchemists were confused by the source of this New World dye. Some thought it came from the seed of the Indian fig, or prickly pear cactus; others correctly identified it as being from an insect that housed itself in the Indian fig. The insects that became known as cochineal were related to the European kermes, but ten times as productive. The harvesting of kermes fell out of favor, while importing America's cochineal became a profitable enterprise.

There are further hints that the liqueur came to Italy before the monks set up shop at Santa Maria Novella. There is proof of an eighth-century tonic called *confectio alchermes* in the 1728 Cyclopaedia. Its recipe reads something like a potion for black magic. Not only did this concoction include rosewater and orange blossom, but it also contained raw silk, apple juice, ground pearls, musk, ambergris, and gold leaf along with the cinnamon, sugar, and honey. In old annals of medicine, *confectio alchermes* was considered one of the best cardiacs, frequently prescribed for palpitations of the heart, sometimes for smallpox and measles, and always as a general restorative.

Regardless of who initially created the liqueur, it did find great favor during the rule of the Medicis. From reading my medieval cookbook, I imagine the flavor of alkermes enhancing many sweet dishes at court. It was also known as the Elisir di Lunga Vita (Elixir of Long Life) and was introduced into French society by Catherine de' Medici as a liqueur to be drunk in small cut-crystal glasses, where it best refracted its own light. Queen Catherine championed the drink as a must-have for any royal cellar. I, of course, became so enamored of the idea of Catherine's elixir that I had to find a real bottle to taste at least once. The story read too ripely for me not to want to track it down.

I soon rued the day that I did not buy a bottle of alkermes long ago in that apothecary shop in Florence, because it proved otherwise impossible to find. This is before Santa Maria Novella opened a shop in New York, where these days you can readily get alkermes—I think it rather a pity that the converted do not need to work a little harder these days. We had no plans to go back to Florence anytime soon. We gravitated to southern Italy on a journey of exploration that would take several years to unfold, and I knew just enough about Italian regionality to know that I would be hard-pressed to find a Tuscan delicacy in the southern atmospheres of Puglia, or Campania, or Calabria.

## III

We are driving through the spring green hills of Lucania, or Basilicata, the anklebone of the Italian boot. Alkermes is far from mind; I would not expect to find alkermes in these southern reaches, so far from the domes and terracotta of Florence. It is our first time across these lush Lucanian hills. We were expecting hot, dry dust in these parts. Perhaps in summer, the mountains brown and the earth offers itself up as the primary element; but now, in April, the fruit trees blossom white and fragrant, and the rocky meadows are verdant with grasses, herbs, and wild chicory. Sheep dot the hillsides and move in unison. The sheepdogs—white, furry, and seemingly docile—are lying in the grass next to their flock, watching.

We travel to a small town in the Lucanian Alps, which are rather high and rugged. Most people think of palm trees and seaside when they think of southern Italy, but much of it is given to wild, toothy mountains where the living is hard and isolated. We travel with a friend who has come to Italy for the first time to retrace her roots. Both her grandmother and grandfather left the same village over a hundred years ago, though they left separately and didn't meet or marry until arriving in the United States and settling in Chicago. Theirs is one of the many thousands of Italian immigrant stories that created our country. All immigrant tales share similarities in the broad strokes, yet their particular details differ.

Our friend Antonia is both nervous and excited to finally be making this trek. The first person in her family for more than a hundred years to return, she has imagined barren hillsides and extreme poverty, the world painted by the difficulties of southern Italy at the end of the 1800s, the world her ancestors fled. She is stunned by the plenty we see growing all around us.

When we turn off the major highway toward Antonia's village, the road climbs. We stop at the bottom of the hill to take Antonia's photograph for posterity by the sign for her town, Trevigno, Three Vines. We stop again, this time at a bend in the road to look at a flock of sheep; also for Antonia to catch her breath and collect herself before we pass through the gates. Return is always marked by a sober rooting of oneself in the past. Any return of this kind becomes important.

A shepherd dressed in a tweed jacket and a wool cap ambles toward us, his big shepherd's crook reminding us incongruously of Little Bo Peep. Antonia had told us that her grandmother was a shepherdess in these very hills. Antonia pats the white sheepdog that looks uncannily like her own two dogs at home, then grazes her arm by accident on the dog's collar, as spiked and ominous-looking as some medieval torture instrument. The collar is supposed to protect the dog from the local wolves, which, in lunging for his jugular, would be sorely surprised. There is now an abrasion on Antonia's arm, the skin having broken. The spiked collar has drawn blood, but the injury is slight.

We walk into the small square of the out-of-the-way village and look at the faces of the men sitting on benches lined against the walls of houses and shops. Antonia sees her own father in the bone structure, the eyes, and the thick hair covering these old men's crowns. In the Bar Centrale where we go for a coffee and to begin the foray into the oral history of Antonia's family, I see traces of Antonia's own face in the woman *barista* behind the counter. The broad shape of the cheekbones and the lighter coloring of the skin are features they share. Caleb begins to ask questions to facilitate Antonia's introduction. This small village does not get much traffic from the outside world; the bar bristles with silence. We feel we are in one of those dated spaghetti westerns where the outlaws come into the saloon and are met with quiet suspicion. I notice to my discomfort that several of the women and men, including the *barista,* are staring at me specifically. I wonder if it is my paler skin or the blond streaking through my hair, for I would never be mistaken for Italian despite how hard I might try to master the language and to blend in.

One gentleman in the bar, Roberto, takes charge. He is a dapper older man with an angelic smile; he has traveled to the United States before and even had relatives, like Antonia, come visit him here. They were also from

Chicago, which he pronounces *Ki-Cago, ch* in Italian being a hard sound rather than soft. A small man behind him shouts, "Ki-Cago! Bang-bang! Al Capone!" The tension lifts as we all laugh together.

As the laughter subsides, we are offered drinks on the house. Antonia is hailed as a local daughter, and there is an easy ebb and flow of questions and answers and more questions. After we share our story of where we are from and why we are here, the *barista* sighs with relief. She shakes her head and tells us that when we walked in, everyone thought they were seeing a ghost. I had been mistaken for another prodigal of the village, the daughter of a woman who had left for France several years ago, and whom they imagined would stay in France and never return. Antonia, Caleb, and I laugh together, for I am the most unlikely of Italians. To be thought of as a child of people in these parts—trumping Antonia, the true Italian among us—seems absurd.

We walk through the town with Roberto, meanwhile translating Antonia's questions about her family. It seems that her last remaining relative in the village has just recently died, but Roberto works hard to think of possible cousins and distant relations. Perhaps the postman is related to Antonia's grandmother, perhaps the baker is related by marriage. Roberto assures us we will find the connections and that an appointment will be made at the town hall to look at birth, marriage, and death records, to make better sense of the scattering of facts in Antonia's family tree that she has brought with her.

After a homecoming drink of homemade wine with

Roberto and his wife in their neat and tidy home, we buy bread and *taralle,* small ring-shaped biscuits scented with anise, from the baker. In every face, we search for the tell-tale signs of Antonia's family, and also I find that I cannot help but search for my own. Do I have some lost genetic trace, far from my Irish, Swiss, and Swedish roots, nestled here in these ragged mountains?

Antonia is spooked. Up the stairs of an old palazzo where her relations apparently had lived for hundreds of years, she sees a plaque with her family name on the door of the apartment of her recently deceased last remaining relative. She takes a photo.

We unwittingly follow two schoolgirls fresh from the hair salon to the local *alimentari.* Their thick light brown hair is styled neatly and exactly the same, the ends flipped and grazing their shoulders. While we look for jams and honeys to take home, and a piece of cheese for a snack, the girls buy nylon stockings. We imagine that they must have a dance this evening. Will they dress up in silk frocks and meet up with boys who are brushed, gelled, and suited to please them? Here in this town, Saturday-evening court-ship will follow the same pattern and rules that have been in place ever since the Middle Ages.

We scan the shelves for local products. We are always on the hunt for the native bottle of bitters or *eau de vie.* My hand traces the usual national brand names on the bottles before me, and then I gasp in surprise, thinking I must sound a little like a heroine in a bad melodrama. There before me is the unexpected. I have come to the end of a quest in this small grocery in a village far from everything.

I almost feel as if I have found my own long-lost relative. There before me is a carmine-colored bottle of alkermes.

## IV

Many years after our journey to Trevigno, my husband and I have moved the location of our restaurant upstairs to a small hidden space above our old digs. Above a false window that we have hung with gauze curtains and twinkling star-shaped lights, we've put a shelf for displaying various bottles of wine, a nod to another experience in another foreign country. Once in the city of Buenos Aires we had lunch in a cozy restaurant whose walls were lined with high shelves of standing bottles of wine. Storing bottles this way is horrible for the wine (and means you can't rotate the bottles frequently), but the effect is jaunty. There was something romantic about the waiter who said we must drink the best bottle in the house and reached up above us for a lovely Malbec that cost us lucky-in-exchange Americans less than five dollars.

At our restaurant in Vermont, the bottle of alkermes unearthed in Trevigno now sits next to a friend's pool hall trophy in red and gold, which Caleb likes to keep at the restaurant so our place looks like all those narrow Italian bars with the local kids' soccer trophies mixed in with the Campari and whisky. It is a detail that encourages questions from the patrons. Sometimes I tell the truth, that it is a friend's billiard trophy and he likes to show it off here, or sometimes I pull that truth a little out of shape and jokingly claim the trophy for my own—international snooker champion that I am, didn't you know?

The bottle had pride of place beside the trophy, yet sometimes we forgot it was even there. Sometimes we looked up to remember, and plotted how we would use it in a dessert. But both Caleb and I were reluctant to pour the liqueur, because then it would be gone.

Yet one afternoon while working on a menu for a wine-tasting dinner, we were stumped about what to serve with the Tuscan dessert wine. In recent dinners, we had already done pear tarts, apple cakes, almond biscotti. We were looking for something different. Our Tuscan friend Luisa had just recently spied the bottle of alkermes on the shelf, and she had given us the recipe for her mother's alkermes cream tart. Looking at the crimson bottle, we considered this offering. We were hesitant, but we decided it was silly to keep saving the bottle, especially since it was becoming so much more readily available. Our reasoning: We should use the alkermes, partake of it, in the way we use our best china every day rather than saving the plates, teacups, and saucers for the special occasion that is never special enough. Alkermes is meant to be imbibed, not coveted like a museum piece. The liqueur is just another example of the living history for which we are always searching.

Caleb thought of another recipe, the one for *pan di spagna*, an egg-white sponge cake made by nuns since a long time ago. We could slice the cake in the middle, soak the pieces in the alkermes, and layer the cake with fresh whipped cream.

The dinner went off with the excitement and fanfare of special dishes paired with special wines. Soaked into the cake, the alkermes tasted slightly sweet and of candied roses and violets. There was also something indescribable that tasted *red*—as if a color had flavor. I loved retelling the story of historical alkermes at tableside, that in the Renaissance the brilliant red came from carmine in lady-bugs' wings. (I actually glided by where the color comes from in our modern era. My research has suggested to me that this is no Red Dye No. 9, and that it is still connected to its origins and made like it has always been made.)

Now the alkermes is gone. As at the end of any good meal, or good story, we suffer a bit of postpartum depression. I think I'll order another bottle from the Santa Maria Novella store, now in Manhattan, but somehow this seems like cheating. Instead, I think we'll make this the subject of another quest the next time we travel in Italy—always searching for the elusive delicacy. Or I will try to make it myself. I will seek out the ingredients: orange blossom, rosewater, cinnamon, honey, ambergris, ground pearls, and Peruvian cochineal. I will be like Rene Le Florentin, setting up a small *alembic*—a chemical apparatus with a wide bottom, like a wine decanter—in my barn to distill my concoctions. I, too, will become an alchemist searching for a different kind of gold.

◡◠

### recipe for *pan di spagna*, using alkermes

Pan di spagna, or Spanish bread, is a traditional "keeping cake" born out of the medieval convent kitchen. Because of the egg whites, this cake has incredible longevity (hence the "keeping" quality), and while it is delicious served fresh and spongy, I like it left to dry. Then it soaks up the liquid and flavor of the alkermes all the better.

4 eggs, separated
1¼ cups sugar
1 teaspoon vanilla extract
Zest of 1 lemon
1 cup flour, sifted
Alkermes liqueur, for bathing the cake
Fresh whipped cream
Mint or rose garnish, if you like

Butter and flour an 8-inch cake pan, and preheat the oven to 350 degrees F. Beat the egg yolks and sugar until ribbony, then add the vanilla and lemon zest and mix thoroughly. Add the flour and mix it in thoroughly but gently; hard mixing will toughen the batter and the texture of the final cake. Let the batter rest while you whip the egg whites until they are just stiff, but still soft and not dry. Using your bare hand, mix one-third of the egg whites into the batter, taking care to break up the yellow cake mixture and saturate it with the whites. Add another third of the whites and mix it in gently but thoroughly. Finally, fold in the remaining whites, leaving streaks of whites through-out the batter. Fill the cake pan to a depth of 1 inch, and level the batter out in the pan. Bake for 30 to 40 minutes, or until a small knife comes out clean and the cake has just pulled away from the insides of the pan. Let the cake rest for 10 or 15 minutes, then remove it from the pan and let it cool completely. For serving, you can spoon a little of the alkermes over each slice and garnish with fresh whipped cream. Another way to present the dessert is to pour some liqueur in a shallow dish, cut each portion in half horizontally, dip the cut face of the bottom half in the liqueur, place it on the serving plate with some whipped cream on it, then dip the cut face of the top half in the liqueur and place it on top, thus completing the portion. Add a dollop of whipped cream on top. Garnish with a sprig of mint or rose petals and serve.

⌐⁊

### recipe for alkermes manhattan

Recently, I had a conversation over our wine bar with a friend who is part of the well-loved Blue Ribbon collection of restaurants in New York City. While I plied him with a Tuscan pizza and tastes of a gamay and rare varietal cornelin from the Val d'Aosta we talked of the magic of alkermes. An ardent fan of this Florentine liqueur, our friend revealed some of the mystery of their alkermes manhattan served in the city.

- 2 ounces Old Overholt rye (just like for the Sazerac)
- ½ ounce alkermes (the one made by Santa Maria Novella, based in Firenze, but with a retail store on Lafayette St in NYC.)

The two alcohols should be stirred with ice and served up in a chilled rocks glass (but no rocks) with two Luxardo

Maraschino cherries. This makes a really fantastic manhattan, the liquore filling the space normally occupied by the two ingredients vermouth and bitters. It's important that the main staple be rye rather than bourbon, as the alkermes does have a fair amount of sugar, and the bourbon will be too sweet.

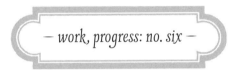

## — work, progress: no. six —

Autumn has arrived. In just a matter of days the leaves have changed from green to yellows, oranges, and bright reds. Golden yellow mixes with the more saturated colors. The air has been warm during the day, and the weather calm. No more wild winds or remnants of hurricanes. No rain.

The drive to New Haven north of Middlebury, Vermont, is stunning on a Wednesday morning. The roads are not too crowded or too slow yet (though soon there will be plenty of rubbernecking, out-of-state Sunday drivers who come to look at the "foliage"). The gap road from Hancock to East Middlebury is washed out in places and under construction, the surface uneven and pebbled, half dirt and half tarmac. The light filters through the branches of the trees.

I go to New Haven to pick grapes. There is now another dimension to harvest here in Vermont. We are not just picking apples, threshing hay, cutting down corn. All over the state, in little pockets of land, small vineyards gather volunteers and paid workers with yellow harvest baskets who clip bunches of grapes that then get crushed and pressed.

At Lincoln Peak, the vineyard where we've bought our own rootstock, they have been picking for a week now. I've just missed the harvest of the Marquette grapes, the dark red grape that is a cross between a *Vitis vinifera* cultivar descended from Pinot Noir and our own native *V. riparia.* There is great excitement about this grape, a relatively new creation. This will be the first year that Chris Granstrom, the winemaker and owner at Lincoln Peak, will make a single varietal wine with his Marquette. Last year, his first vintage, he made his Cove Road from a blend of Marquette, St. Croix, and Frontenac. No one knows yet what this Marquette grape can do, for it is too young for any testing to ascertain its tannic structure and longevity. The harvest of Chris's Marquette grapes went seamlessly, and the fruit seems perfect with an ideal *Brix,* or sugar content. There is a great sense of anticipation.

Today, we are picking La Crescent, a white grape created from Riesling. I go to work in the vineyard with my back to the sun, and I can feel its strength on the back of my neck. The hot air smells of ripe peaches. Wasps buzz about my hands when I reach into the leafy vine to clip. On this particular stretch of vine, the leaves have not been as aggressively pruned, and I have to pull out vegetation to get to the clusters. These grapes have seen a bit too much of the rain we had this summer, and I have to look carefully at each bunch to weed out what's called sour rot or gray rot. The grapes on certain bunches look shriveled and smell like vinegar; yet not all shriveled grapes are rotten. Some are just raisinated, or drying and sweet, and, for this wine, that's fine. I constantly taste the grapes to gauge what is good and what isn't. My small red-handled pruners snip, and when I toss the bunches in my yellow basket, they make a pleasing soft thud. The vineyard is quiet with just this occasional dull noise, the sound of my shears snipping, my own breathing, and the cackles of agitated rooks punctuating the morning until I hear the call for lunch across the hill.

Lunch is taken on two picnic benches near the tasting room in the shade of a maple tree. It's warm enough out that the shade feels good, and all of us unfold sandwich papers or open containers for our midday meal. I share a table with a young woman named Tara. She is "up from Boston" and has spent the last couple of years living and traveling abroad: London, Dublin, Africa. A young man, Blair, sits next to me. He and his wife have recently moved to Vermont from Tucson via New York City. They were looking for a place to resettle, and each time they opened a map, their eyes kept wandering to Vermont. Between jobs, both Tara and Blair answered ads for jobs picking grapes that the vineyard had posted on Craigslist. A man who came here to Vermont from Brooklyn over twenty years ago sits across from me. He's getting out of his woodshop, getting out of the sawdust, picking grapes to be outdoors.

After lunch, I meet Chris in the *cantina*. His Marquette must is already fermenting in the big stainless-steel tanks he imported from Italy. He tells me he is changing some of his techniques with this wine this year. He is keeping the tanks cooler for the first fermentation to moderate the fruit a bit. Once a strawberry farmer, he declares the soil here very loamy and actually "too good" for growing grapes. But this is the land that he has, so he adjusts his work in the vineyard and *cantina* accordingly.

The Marquette is a fairly aggressive grower. After the first year of planting the grapes close together to make them compete with the earth for nutrients (grapes like to work hard), Chris realized this just made a mare's nest of the vines and bunches. He pulled out every other vine to give the Marquette a little more rambling room, and trained the vines by what's called the Geneva Curtain System: The vine grows in the center of a three-wired "roof" row, reaching up to trellis both backward and forward along the wires. Such a shape makes for easier pruning, ripening, and picking. Chris likes to grow his grapes up a bit higher so that they are not touched by a late May frost, or by the roaming wild turkeys.

I am invited to taste barrel samples of all the early fermenting wines, turning the spigots on the big steel tanks to catch a little of the liquid, in turn, into a small beaker glass. The glass is part of the paraphernalia of a chemist, and I feel a little lost, for I am no chemist. Molecules and compounds escape me. I taste by intuition. I taste each one carefully. This tastes clean. This one tastes like the grape still on the vine. This one tastes like a green apple, suggesting that a more advanced fermentation has yet to begin. I have not yet trained myself to know that this flavor (and its aroma) is 3-methylbutanoate, which naturally develops in the course of alcoholic fermentation.

Two young men drive the tractor down to the *cantina*. The tractor pulls a flatbed piled with the yellow baskets full of our morning's work. Often, the bunches of grapes get rotated through a special machine called a crusher. This process separates the grapes from the stems. The softly crushed and destemmed grapes then get processed in the presser. With the La Crescent, Chris has decided to skip the crusher and press the whole bunches first. With white grapes, the crusher can cause bitterness in the wine because the juice will have had too much contact with the grape skins. The baskets get weighed, then dumped into the large horizontal cylinder of the presser. When the presser is turned on, a large plastic bag inside inflates and presses out all the juice; it's then transported through a network of hoses into the fermentation tank. This process is quicker and simpler than that of the old wooden cider press borrowed from a neighbor that we will use to press our own first harvest until we can afford to buy something of our own.

I return to the vineyard to pick. This stretch of La Crescent has been trained as a Double Geneva Curtain and has been well pruned. The picking goes quickly, and I find that many fewer bunches have been affected by the rain. The sun casts an oblique angle of light across the vines in the meadow, cloaking us all in a honeyed aura that I imagine is much like the wine the La Crescent will make. The bunches of grapes glow against their green leaves. When I taste the fruit, I can taste the mother Riesling in the La

Crescent, the peach fruit note and the floral linden tree blossom that I always mistake for gardenia or oleander. I clip a bunch, almost perfect, to take home for Caleb to taste.

The pickers who were here the day before have all encouraged me to find a rogue bunch of Marquette to taste. Two of the vineyard workers, whose names I do not know, find a dark, ripe bunch, clip it, and put it in my hands. All that fruit feels heavy. I pick a grape and taste. A rush of blackberry and raspberry, bright and brambly. This bunch, too, I will take home. One of the young men asks me if this is my first time picking. "Yes," I say, though somehow I feel as if I've done this before. The snipping, tasting, and handpicking feels completely natural. The young man tells me this is his second year. Last year, after the harvest, he went around and picked all the red bunches that had been missed and made his own wine. (I wonder if he called it Rogue Red.)

Chris gives me a bottle of last year's La Crescent to take home. I want to taste some to bring the whole process neatly to a conclusion. How rare that one finds such closure to an experience guided by nature. After the drive back to my own parcel of land, the sun has already fallen behind the spine of the Chateauguay just a little above us. In the gray evening light, I set out my two bunches of grapes, one red and one white, to admire on our own tasting table. Caleb and I eat the fruit together, then open our bottle of Chris's gift of La Crescent. We marvel at the fact that this wine was grown and made here in Vermont. It tastes more than good. It tastes venerable. The wine shows all the earmarks of an off-dry Riesling—the full body, the same fruit and floral aromas that we taste in the actual fruit, the same orange blossom and citrus that occur after Riesling has been in the bottle for a while. And there is that distinct oily scent typical of Riesling and the acidity that draws out the flavors.

I go out into my own fledgling and experimental vineyard and look at my five rows of vines. All except one look healthy and vibrant. It's time we properly trellised them before the winter arrives, so they will be supported come spring. We should allow them one more year of growth before we expect them to produce; but if we are lucky, and if these grapes like our dense clay soil, come their second spring they will flower, and a few grapes will be born. They will show us the promise of the year after that, then the year after that, and the succession of the years to come.

– 7 –

*with me and drink as I*

Drink with me, and drink as I.

Modern society is in danger of shutting out the garden of its senses . . . two senses of which our appreciation is in decline: taste and smell.

MAX LEGLISE

*La Chasse aux Papillons:* the hunt for the butterflies. I look at the name on my perfume bottle procured in Paris just a couple of years ago to be sure I have spelled this title correctly even though I studied French for fourteen years. The bottle is narrow and edged like a hexagon, and has a label, a thin vertical pink strip of color with the name embossed in gold, and a heavy hexagonally shaped gold top that calls to mind a large cocktail ring. The shape and elements of the bottle don't surprise me, the perfume industry seeming so closely aligned with that other sensuous adornment, jewelry. At the same time, this bottle greatly differs from those I usually handle—those smooth broad-shouldered wine bottles that I unpack from delivery boxes, or pull from racks to serve. But somehow, in that they hold liquids that please the nose and that require fastidious care in their making, I think these two kinds of bottles might not be so different after all.

I am contemplating butterflies and this bottle of perfume because we are in a storm of butterflies here at home, monarchs and fritillaries resting and drinking deeply in our perennial garden and mint hedge. Vermont's end of summer is hot, and the butterflies have landed on every available floral surface. They stay their wings, pressing them close together so they become almost two-dimensional, or look as if they are praying. The orange and black palette of the monarch overrides the small black-winged fritillaries with their bits of red and orange embroidered in the dust of their armature. Science—or is it myth—says that the beating wings of butterflies in South America can affect the weather in China.

Did the *parfumeur* who created my butterfly perfume experience a similar flight of monarchs? Did he also see fields full of butterfly hunters? Dressed in white shirts with long sleeves, white pants, and pith helmets or wide-brimmed straw hats, they walk through the tall, straw-colored grass of the adjacent meadow with their nets poised. My husband and I cannot help but think this is a scene out of a Henry James novel or a Merchant-Ivory film, a moment when the party stops in the meadow with picnic and parasols, stifled in their heavy clothes in the yellowed August heat.

I am transported back to a hot day in Paris. On its stone-paved streets, I am walking briskly. The air feels so warm that the season is misleading. This could be late August in Paris, yet it is only mid-April. I am crossing the street from the Louvre to the Rue de Rivoli, which is known mostly for its shaded arcade and its chocolate shop Angeline, where the tourists go to drink cups of thick chocolate on chilly spring days or damp fall evenings. I am not going to the arcade; I am not going to Angeline. I have another purpose altogether. I am going to a perfume shop.

At the beginning of Rue de Rivoli where the street is wide and devoid of trees, the heat beats on me unrelentingly. I turn down a perpendicular street, the Amiral Coligny, then slip into a small storefront with huge plate glass windows that look out onto the busy midmorning traffic and the gray walls of that Baroque monolith, the Louvre. The shop is stark and cool even though the sun pours through the windows. Taut linen shades pulled halfway down still let in plenty of light, yet help keep the space from heating up too much. The walls are white, and the floors look like ancient pine polished to a high gloss. For all I know, these floors are so old that Queen Marie Antoinette might have stood here, too. I have been sent to this little boutique by two friends, one who lives across the ocean, and the other who lives here in the city. The shop is called L'Artisan Parfumeur.

Even though the space feels cooler inside, sweat still lines my upper lip and I feel a bit self-conscious when confronting the comfortable, dry chic of the young salesman. He immediately asks if he can help. I smile hopefully and tell him I am looking for a "signature scent." Or at least something that will seep into my skin and mix well with my own chemistry, something that I can make my own. His eyes brighten—this must be one of his favorite tasks, to help a client find a scent that speaks without saying a word, a scent that has promising *sillage*—the word the French use for the light drift of scent that precedes a person into a room, and that follows in a person's wake, barely discernible and intriguing.

I stand in the light-filled shop. As I have at many junctures in my life, I wonder how I arrived here in this place at this time. Often I've stopped myself, practically in midstep, and thought: *How did I study literature and film in college, and end up owning a restaurant? How did I spend so many years studying French and find myself living in Italy? How did I become a writer, and also become a serious student of wine? How did I end up in this small perfume shop when I came to Paris as a restaurateur?* The answer to this last question is that I believe perfume is the flip side of my passion for wine and liqueur. My understanding of perfume will be crucial to the development of my nose and palate, not only as a sommelier, but also as a winemaker and *maître liquoriste.*

My journey to this point began innocently enough, on a cold, windblown March night in New York City when Caleb and I dined with two friends whom we had met years before when we still had a bakery. Josh, at that time, was a food and wine writer, and his wife, Ellen, was a photographer specializing in food. A long time had passed since we had met over a pastry counter, and Josh had since changed professions. Ellen still worked in her Manhattan studio; and even though Josh no longer wrote about food and wine, this change had not diminished his wine collection, nor the "cellar" he had created. This cellar fascinated me. He had fashioned it out of silver-faced foam insulation, a condenser, and duct tubing, all working in concert in what had once been a front hall coat closet in their apartment on Riverside Drive.

The narrow sliver of a space was now packed from floor to ceiling with wine. Each bottle had a collar on the neck on which Josh had written the name of the wine and its vintage. I was immediately envious of his perfectly cataloged system, thinking of my incessant battle in managing my own cellar at the restaurant. I can never keep a fully up-to-date inventory because I am always distracted by investing in more wine. Wine is always arriving, and the wine racks in the office, and in my temperature-controlled wine refrigerators, and in the storage compartment under the wine bar, are always full. I have run out of space for wine, with boxes stored under the long banquette, stacked in a tiny alcove to the entrance of the restaurant, and even—to the dismay of our business neighbors with whom we share a vestibule—camping in a pile outside our door.

It takes a long time for me to inventory all this wine; and once I get started, of course, the inventory constantly changes. Diners drink wine at dinner. Empty bottles fill the wooden recycling container that goes down with us at the end of the evening below our restaurant porch, when we cross paths with the little skunk. (The skunk likes to investigate under the staircase leading up to the restaurant.) Of course, I complicate matters by ordering new wine to replace what I've sold, in addition to bringing in new bottles to refine the list. I rely heavily on my good, but not-exactly-photographic, visual memory to recall where I've squirreled away which wine. When one of our patrons places an order, or I've suggested a specific vintage, sometimes I catch myself wondering—for a moment—*Where is it?* Even with the great improvement of making my own collars for the wines after that dinner at Josh and Ellen's, my system must resemble a madman's stockpile to the naïve outsider. I confess I envy those sleek temperature-controlled wine rooms in the latest-designed restaurants where all the wine is kept in bins, and the wine list labels the bin number next to the wine for the ease of anyone in search of the bottle.

That night at dinner with Josh and Ellen, we tasted some aged bottles that Josh had been waiting for the right occasion to uncork. I have to say, for one of the first times in my life, I remember nothing of the wine, which is a disgrace because I know the bottles were all quite good, and there were vintages offered that I will probably never have an opportunity to taste again. I had became side-tracked, too entranced by Josh's wine cellar, and I was thinking about how I could employ his methods. If such a distraction was not enough, Josh made a comment that changed, or I should say *distilled,* my thinking about wine. While we sat contemplating the contents of our glasses, he said, offhandedly yet seriously, "I'm really just a frustrated *parfumeur.*" *Parfumeur,* I thought. I knew exactly what he meant: This whole process of tasting wine, deconstructing and rebuilding a wine from our noses and palates alone, really was work closely related to that of a *parfumeur,* who also manipulates raw ingredients, attuned to every nuance of methodology, to achieve an exquisite combination.

We talked of perfume and wine, and the perfume of wine, for a good part of our evening, which ran very late into the night. Josh spoke of a *parfumeur* in Paris, a de rigueur boutique, where you could go smell the various scents that had been created. He spoke of the shop as a catalog of scent where you could take in all the elements of the concoction. Caleb and I would be in Paris soon, so at once I imagined making a pilgrimage.

L'Artisan works like a museum of scent. At L'Artisan, the natural framework of the light and the plain walls with the warm, honeyed tones of the wood floor provide a clean tabula rasa for the intricacy of the fragrances. The various scents of the perfumes that L'Artisan makes are lined up in small votive-shaped glasses on a freestanding chest-high partition. Muslin saturated with the perfumes is contained in the glasses. You dip your nose into the glass, just as you would when smelling wine. You may smell the perfumes either in the order of their presentation—which follows a pattern of floral, fruity, earthy, spicy—or you may smell them at random. You may smell again and again. On a quiet weekday morning, the salesman is delighted to act as guide, and to talk about the various notes and ingredients of each perfume.

L'Artisan Parfumeur was created in 1976 by Jean Laporte, one of the "great noses" of France. His paternal grand-mother, deeply interested in botany, taught him how to evaluate flower, leaf, and fruit aromas. These first impres-sions from his childhood were the impetus for his stud-ies and training to become a *parfumeur*. His idea was to promote fragrance's artistic values as well as its traditional ones, a creative concept that favored unusual fragrance notes using mostly natural ingredients. This was a depar-ture from the precepts of the modern perfume industry that developed at the turn of the nineteenth century. Most created scents were made from a chemistry of synthetics, which had produced a democracy of scent. Anybody could buy a good perfume, and all industry perfumes were standardized. True musk comes from the glands of a rare deer in the Himalayas. It is, of course, much cheaper and easier to create artificially the molecules that make up this deer's special musk than to trek to the far reaches of the world and risk one's own life as well as take the life of an almost extinct four-footed creature.

Yet synthetic is synthetic, and sounds unappealing even if it can smell good. Laporte's concept was to revert to using the best of a small natural harvest. Not only was this a departure, but it also represented a return to the origin of perfumes created from the distilled essential oils of flowers and herbs. Jean-François Laporte eventually left his initial creation and went on to revive the historical concept of a perfumery by creating Maître Parfumeur et Gantier, which continued to use only the rarest and best raw materials. In this way, he developed a luxurious and very expensive perfume line based on traditional recipes of the seventeenth century. The aristocracy of perfume revived.

To create any fragrance, a Master *Parfumeur* draws on a variety of inspirations informed by a sense of place and narrative. One of the perfumes on display in the L'Artisan boutique perfectly illustrated the process. Master *Parfumeur* Bertrand Duchaufour, intrigued by what he called the "real" perfumes of Africa, traveled there frequently to try to find the source of rich scents that were apparently never quite the same, but never entirely different. In his pursuit of these elusive scents, his travels took him as far as Mali, where the secret was finally revealed in the traditional art of *wusulan*. *Wusulan* is the Malian art of making perfume—an art that has been handed down through generations from mother to daughter, the aim being to seduce and keep your beloved. A hint of floral fragrances is added to macerations of wood, roots, and resins that, when heated, produce fragrant curls of smoke. The perfume Duchaufour created in response to and in honor of *wusulan* is named Timbuktu, the result a bewitching and many-layered alchemy recalling the European response to what it christened "the mystery" of the African continent. There are top notes of green mango; the center focuses on the fragrance of the karo karoundé flower, which is full of herbs and spice. The bottom notes are both piquant and balmy, reminiscent of the smell of heat on human skin. The whole fragrance exudes wild iris and vetiver as well as the myrrh of African earth.

I am finding it difficult to choose the perfect scent. There is the ritual: first of smelling each perfume alone, detecting the different notes in its recipe, then trying each perfume on my own skin. (You put a spritz on the skin of your inner arm, moving up the arm, patch by patch of fragrance.) The compounds creating each scent react differently with a person's individual chemistry, creating a harmony or a discord. The salesman does not rush me; he expects me to try the different perfumes that attract me in their pure form. He encourages me to walk around the shop for a bit with each scent emanating from my skin, because the aromas will change given time.

As I perambulate, I eye beautifully packaged lotions and candles. The drawer sachets are made of a fabric that looks like a linen organza. My gaze rests on a special display for a special perfume. In front of me is L'Artisan's Vintage Perfume for this year, Fleur de Narcissus. *A vintage perfume*, I think. This is a new approach to making and advertising perfume: to focus on the beauty of natural, raw materials in its creation—and to concentrate the year, region, culture, grand cru, and rarity in its lineage. A vintage perfume from a specific region and specific site creates a new reverence and attention for the fragrances. Enthusiasts can collect these limited and rare issues of perfume just as the oenophile collects rare varietals and blends. L'Artisan has boldly followed in the path of the vineyard by making these small-batch, organic perfumes that are dated, bottled, and marketed like wine.

I have the good fortune to be able to talk to the woman who is the current creative director of the perfumes. Petite, with long, dark curly hair, she looks to be a young fifty, dressed for the heat in a simple camisole. She has lovely wrinkles by her eyes as she smiles. She is both the house *parfumeur* and a visionary. Her approach to the perfume is just like a winemaker's. She talks of scent, aroma, aging, extraction, and *terroir*. We buzz back and forth, our conversation echoing each other's thoughts. My friend has told me that L'Artisan can formulate a true "signature scent" for a client, a concoction specific to the buyer and unique. I inquire about what this might entail. I am inspired when the house *parfumeur* replies that this long process involves initial interviews during which the client answers dozens of personal questions that give a well-rounded impression of his or her personality. What's your favorite color? Favorite film? Book? What do you like to cook? What is your favorite vacation destination? The list of questions is pages long. From these answers, she pairs the client with another *parfumeur*. Most *parfumeurs* work freelance or for an international organization called the IFF (International Flavors and Fragrances), even though they may be in-house creators of scents for couture, cosmetic, and jewelry houses. L'Artisan's *parfumeur* believes that the correct match of freelance *parfumeur* and client is crucial to the success of the signature scent.

Once the chosen *parfumeur* has met the client, read over the list of answers, and asked more questions, he or she gathers various single-note scents—orange blossom, white tea, musk, violet, and so on—that correspond to the client's interests and personality. Several additional meetings ensue so that the client can smell the various notes and respond. The *parfumeur* takes the results of those meetings and keeps some scents, throws out others. Then, at last clear on what pleases the client's olfactory senses, the *parfumeur* begins to weave the elements of scent together to make a tapestry evoking the client's personality. The *parfumeur* and client meet again several times to smell these perfume *essaies,* or sketches, and refine the distillate. The creation of the perfume can take upward of a year and is a careful choreography of *parfumeur* as artist and muse.

Such an arduous process may seem extravagant to us in the twenty-first century, but this is how all perfume was at one time created—scents were blended for a specific person, who would then always be associated with that fragrance. This anointing with scent goes back even farther than the creation of distillations to drink. In fact, the crafting of artisanal, alcoholic beverages grew out of the process of creating essential oils and perfumes, and the two have always seemed to go hand and glove throughout history. I say *glove* deliberately. Our modern idea of perfume was established by Catherine de' Medici, that young Italian wife of Henry II of France. She brought that personal *parfumeur,* Renato Bianco, with her to Paris, and kept him very close until she granted him freedom. He was then able to found his own atelier in the narrow streets of his adopted Paris and became one of the first *parfumeurs* to set up shop as uniquely a scent maker. In the Middle Ages and Renaissance, *parfumeurs* were closely associated with glove makers. Fine gloves were soaked in fragrance in order for the noble wearer to be able to hold a finger to the nose and breathe sweetly when so much around him or her was fetid and foul. To attend grand *salons* that smelled intoxicatingly of perfume and leather fed the French culture's obsessive desire for splendor and seduction. Catherine de' Medici, a strong personality moving ahead of her peers, arrived well spoken in any discussion of perfume and liqueurs, and lived at the forefront of both arts during her reign. In my own research into wine, brandies, and perfume, she has always materialized like a phantom ambassador.

Sadly, I do not have a year to spend in Paris, or the minor fortune necessary for creating my own signature scent with one of the *parfumeurs* on the L'Artisan roster. But I can procure a ready-made scent from one of the vials on the chest-height white wall. I have narrowed my choice down to two: La Chasse aux Papillons, which is primarily a white floral, slightly spicy scent, redolent of rose, orange blossom, violet, iris, and white pepper; and Drôle de Rose, which brings to mind a hedge of fragrant rugosa roses. I keep returning to these two perfumes, sniffing, then spritzing. I smell the underside of my own wrist over and over again. I can see my own blue veins pulsing beneath the very thin, fine skin. There are no clocks in the boutique, but I ask the salesman the time. It's time for lunch.

Since I cannot decide, I decide to get both fragrances. La Chasse aux Papillons mixes well with my own chemistry and expresses some of my favorite fragrances. Drôle de Rose I cannot turn down, because of my love for roses and for the rose garden I carefully tend at home. I imagine saving this perfume for hot summer days, guiding me through a walk in my own garden where I can meld with my bourbon and gallica blooms; or wearing this scent in the drab center of winter, when the memory of roses will be most welcome.

A little giddy with perfume, as if I have had too much wine, I also choose to buy something for Caleb, sorry that he hasn't been here with me to drink in these scents. I know he would have been fascinated by the story inherent in these fragrances. With the help of the salesman, I choose out of memory what I think might sit well on Caleb's skin.

For him, I take the Fou d'Absinthe, a woodsy, musky scent thick with green foliage and artemisia. Later, I will read reviews of these two perfumes that label them well-made, but without intrigue. I wonder at the work of the perfume critic, like the wine critic. Perfume, like wine, cannot be sensed in a vacuum. Perfume is best appreciated against the canvas of skin, as scents are a response to a person's heat and chemistry, just as wine is best appreciated with the tastes and scents of food. A wine well-paired with a dish expresses the true purpose of the wine; the matching of notes and texture highlight the essence of both the meal and the drink. A perfume that instinctively weaves itself in and out of a person's natural scent is what creates intrigue and mystery. Without the food, without the body, neither wine nor perfume can be articulated fully.

In hindsight, these fragrances I have chosen, La Chasse aux Papillons and Fou d'Absinthe, seem almost premonitory, as if their highly personal and particular perfumed notes tell both the past and the future of the perfumed person. Perhaps they function as the network of lines on the palm of a hand? Somehow I feel that if I pay enough attention to my senses, my past is honored and my future is foretold.

Vermont's fall rains have come. All day yesterday, the rain came down steadily, saturating the gardens and plumping up the roses, which love this English weather. Today, we wake to mist—*a fine day,* as they say in Ireland. The colors of the leaves on the trees are even more brilliant against the gray backdrop of sky and fog. The maples have turned an orange-yellow tinged with lime green and blushed with red. These are my favorite leaves.

We've made a fire in the woodstove, whose flames through the glass match the color of the maples outside. Yesterday, Jean Lenoir's book *Le Nez du Vin* (The Nose of Wine) arrived in a stiff brown cardboard box, though *book* seems a poor description for what was originally created as a piece of art. Lenoir came from the limestone and white marl region of Burgundy and created *Le Nez du Vin* in 1978, exactly thirty years ago. As someone who grew up in a family that encouraged a passion for wine, he learned the art of taste at a very young age while pouring off the family wine from the cask into the pitcher. In his book he describes that wine as "red . . . deep-hued, and unforgettably fruity." He learned to taste wine at the same time he learned to walk.

Early on in his career as a winemaker he decided that, rather than make wines, he wanted to explore the entire range of subtleties found in wine. He wanted to create a "language" for wine that would enliven what he saw as a dying art. He saw society at risk of losing its connection to its senses, particularly those of scent and taste. He felt that the bounty of the earth should no longer be relegated to colorless liquids and solids used only for necessary nutrition; rather that natural bounty should be honored as the portal to profound sensorial emotions. An artist friend encouraged him to begin approaching universities and other educational institutions with his theories about wine as art, as a subject to be studied with the same attention as music or painting. The French being the French loved the notion, and Lenoir began teaching the first wine-tasting classes in 1978 at La Maison de la Culture in Chalon-sur-Saône. The result of these classes fueled a panoply of questions about the study of taste. Most of what we think is taste is actually smell.

Another artist friend of Lenoir encouraged him to create *Le Nez du Vin* as an art object, a book in which the viewer/smeller could interact with a world of scents and begin to create a language to express the experience. Through an incredible amount of research, Lenoir cataloged fifty-four scents that he felt best described the elements in wine. His approach embraced five categories: fruit, floral, vegetal, animal, and roasted. From those categories, words are associated with the fifty-four scents, which are exact natural and/or chemical compound representations of those fragrances, and the exact molecular structure of those scents found in wine. The language of these scents calls forth not only scent recognition, but also distinct memories of experiences associated with these scents. There is nothing like the whiff of a fragrance to take you back to a specific moment in your life: the smell of candied green apple as you peeled a wrapper at the local penny-candy store; the scent of hot, oily tarmac on a summer day while you were riding your first bike; the yeasty aroma of fresh bread baked by the local *boulanger* your first time in Paris. Suddenly a moment in your life is being played back on your own personal silver screen.

I think that if we learn to read, count, write, sing, why can't we be taught to smell? Why isn't smell as prized as these other skills? Olfaction is a complex sense that enables us to perceive differences in smells and aromas, that allows us fully to taste what we drink and what we eat. Scent is the perception found deep inside our own heads, literally. Behind our nose and eyes, tucked into the most central lobe of our brains, is the *olfactory epithelium,* which detects and deconstructs an odorous molecule or fragrance through direct olfaction. Aroma is the perception of the olfactory epithelium when the volatile molecules of wine or food are in our mouths. We receive this information through *retronasal* olfaction. If you pinch your nose, you will lose this perception and realize how much we use it and need it. All that is left are the most basic sensations of taste: acid, sweet, salty, bitter, and *umami,* that inexpressible sense of depth in flavor. There are other various *trigeminal* sensations as well: thermal, mechanical, and chemical. Flavor is what we understand as the combination of olfactory, gustatory, and trigeminal sensations—adding up to what we call *taste.*

There are more than 350 olfactory receptors in the nose. When a scent arrives at the back of the nasal passage, odiferous molecules work like chemical signals, dissolving in the mucus and merging with proteins in the receptors to generate a whole series of reactions. The chemical message created immediately becomes an electrical message, which gets projected as the form of an image onto the olfactory bulb. That's why when some people smell a fragrance, they see a physical description of that fragrance in their mind's eye. When I *smell* cinnamon in an apple pie, I *see* a cinnamon stick. My friend Colleen smells raspberry in a wine and sees the color red. The scent image is cataloged

into the deepest recesses of the brain and tagged ... ...
memory file. That scent memory will be there for us when
that fragrance comes along again. It might just take some
practice to bring the image to the surface.

Lenoir's belief about the relationship between scent
and language, a belief that the Europeans have embraced
for many years, has been more difficult to introduce on
our shores. In the March 10, 2008, Style Issue of *The New
Yorker,* writer John Lancaster reviewed the book *Perfumes:
The Guide* by Luca Turin and Tania Sanchez using his
interest in wine as a foil for understanding the reviews of
the perfumes in the Turin-Sanchez book. He wrote, "The
idea that your palate and your vocabulary expand simul-
taneously might sound felicitous, but there is a catch.
The words and the references are really useful only to
people who have had the same experiences and use the
same vocabulary: those references are to a shared basis
of sensory experience and a shared language." Lancaster
relied on his healthy skepticism when he drank wine with
others whom he considered to be perhaps overly romantic
in their descriptions of their experiences with wine. He
wrote that he'd had difficulty understanding when certain
wine drinkers would use certain adjectives to describe
everything from aroma to mouthfeel in a wine. In particular, the word *grainy,* when referring to the texture of a
wine, had eluded him. At least until a eureka moment
when he tasted a Languedoc red called Le Pigeonnier from
the European heat-wave year of 2003. The mouthfeel *was*
grainy. Suddenly he'd had a shared sensory experience
and discovered a shared language, exactly the philosophy

that Jean Lenoir has been trying to disseminate for the last thirty years.

*Le Nez du Vin* is a tome to be reckoned with. It comes in an oversize format, a big red cloth-covered book with a cover that operates more like a heavy old door. I can almost hear the squeaking of the hinges. Once opened, the book looks like a miniature perfume boutique. One side of the interior of the book holds the fifty-four aromas in little numbered glass vials with black caps. I, who feel fairly confident in the abilities of my nose, am amazed at the nuances of the scents. I begin with number 19. The little glass bottle's liquid is clear to the eye. As I hold its scent under my nose, I am sure that I smell red raspberry. A bright fruitiness exudes, almost like bubble gum. The scent is very full and reminds me of a fresh raspberry jam made just this summer by a friend. I imagine a super-fruity, almost sour candy, like those intense clear candies called Jolly Ranchers, or that soft candy that is an opaque, pink fruit nougat, and the sides of my tongue salivate in the memory. I read the corresponding card and feel frustrated. The scent is apricot? I sniff again and smell the difference, now that I know the word for the smell, and I imagine a bowl of ripe apricots in a hotel room in Istanbul that a friend once told me about from her travels there.

This happens time and again. I try the next vial. I am sure that this is apple. I smell the ripening Libertys in our own orchard. I am transported back to one of our first apartments when we heated apple cider on the stove with a cinnamon stick and kernels of clove. I have no doubt in my olfactory memory. I look at the card and the fruit depicted looks like two red apples to me. When I flip it over, I am surprised. This scent is peach! Now that I smell again, I can detect the still-warm peach pie, the slightly acetate taste of the fuzzy skin as I bite into it, the sweet taste of a particular dessert wine. I offer the vial to Caleb. He smells watermelon.

I search for apple as a counterpoint. *How* does this smell different? The apple scent is bright and green like a Granny Smith, almost vegetal, much less pronounced when I compare it with the peach. I go back and forth between the two, trying to discern the differences, training my nose to search out the characteristics.

The next round is more successful, and I am quite proud of Caleb's young cousin Claire. While working with us at the restaurant all summer, she has become interested in wine. Almost every night at staff dinner, we pour a couple of wines. We smell, taste, and discuss. We are always training our noses and palates. At the beginning of the summer, Claire couldn't detect any specific scents in the wine. She could smell broad elements like alcohol, or fruit, or spice, but never what kind of fruit, what kind of spice. She would get frustrated when we would go around the table and offer up the images from our smelling and tasting. Of course, she is young, just-college-age, and doesn't have the same fund of experiences from which to draw. Yet within a month, she tasted a glass of Riesling grown in the Piemonte and said, "It smells like acetate, you know, fingernail polish." We laughed, but agreed that it did smell that way, but in a good sense.

That night, I watched her follow the scent of the acetate like a trail. Her expression changed. She was on to something. It was as if she was Gretel and had found the trail of bread crumbs taking her away from the Wicked Witch's house. She pounced on the memory, and the image. "Peach skin!" she blurted out. The smell and the flavor of the Riesling reminded her of biting into the slightly bitter, acidic skin of a ripe, juicy peach.

By the time my *Le Nez du Vin* arrives, her nose has improved greatly, though the red wines she used to be attracted to hold little interest for her these days. She prefers to smell and taste white wine. She wonders if she only thought she liked red because her parents do, and her parents' friends do. I work on a theory as well. I think all young wine drinkers go through this phase, preferring white wines before they can drink red. The whites somehow seem more approachable and friendly. Red wine can be intimidating for the young palate. I went through this same rite of passage myself, drinking only white Burgundy for the first two years of my wine-drinking life. I wonder if in a year's time Claire will have moved on and become a champion of red.

We do a round of the scents after dinner. Claire guesses petroleum for her vial, and black pepper for Caleb's vial. I smell mushroom or truffle in her bottle, and then think Caleb's might also be truffle, or rather truffle instead. I also smell Claire's description of burning rubber. Claire shouts her guesses into the dining room as if we are playing a heated parlor game like Trivial Pursuit. I think this is just the excitement of being able to put words to the scents.

Wine language can seem overwrought and contrived if you yourself don't possess the same vocabulary, but once you begin to accumulate the words, and once you make the connections and distinctions, the language seems completely necessary and natural.

Caleb's not sure of what to think of his bottle, and we all guess that mine is roasted hazelnut. It seems so straightforward compared with the other two. Claire is correct that Caleb's bottle is black pepper. We win points for my vial since we are all correct in ascertaining the scent plays hazelnut. Claire's vial is the showstopper. We learn that the bottle is filled with the scent of coffee. We train our noses by smelling all the scents again, several times, and saying the words that define them, before we screw on the little black caps and put the book away for the night.

I think I understand the inspiration of the Master *Parfumeur* even as I understand the inspiration of the Master Winemaker. I think of my own La Chasse aux Papillons and of the days the monarchs came to perch in our garden. My Master *Parfumeur* must have seen a flight of the same orange-and-black butterflies that I saw landing in our mint and roses. The *parfumeur,* as he travels through the world, draws from image and taste just as much as scent. The *parfumeur,* like a winemaker, pulls from the rare and ephemeral fragrance of an exceptional harvest. Even as the distiller tells a story in a glass, in the nose, and on the tongue that speaks of a specific time, a place, and a people, the *parfumeur* tells a similar story on skin. All journeys, whatever destination, leave shiny shards of memories.

*Parfumeurs* capture fragrances that explore the memories inspiring their creations. *Parfumeurs,* winemakers, and distillers capture the fragrances and aromas radiating from the natural land through the raw materials describing both the cultivated and the wild landscape. Wine and perfume are twin arts, and cousins of the classic, oft-read literature in my bookcase, of the masterpiece hanging in the local museum, of the piece of music performed by the touring chamber trio. Scent and taste allow us to escape, to follow a narrative that resonates both within and outside ourselves.

I cannot leave this thinking without returning to a passage from the book *Brideshead Revisited.* I grew up reading and watching the old PBS series of *Brideshead* because my father wrote his dissertation on Evelyn Waugh. We in my family had to endure or embrace the wry pleasures of Waugh—depending on your point of view—and my father assigned my sisters and me lengthy summer reading lists. I remember the scene vividly in which the narrator, Charles Ryder, and his friend Sebastian Flyte make an inventory of the bottles in Sebastian's ancestral cellar, getting terrifically drunk while making tasting notes. It is one of the most lovely, silly, and graceful passages on wine I've ever read.

> "It is a little, shy wine like a gazelle."
> "Like a leprechaun."
> "Dappled, in a tapestry meadow."
> "Like a flute by still water."
> ". . . And this is a wise old wine."

"A prophet in a cave."

". . . And this is a necklace of pearls on a white neck."

"Like a swan."

"Like the last unicorn."

I raise my glass. Here's to a necklace of pearls on a white neck. Here's to the swan. And here's to the last unicorn.

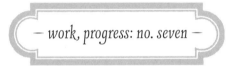

— *work, progress: no. seven* —

The winemaking equipment has arrived. We ordered online an introductory winemaking kit, which comes with all of the necessities: primary fermentation container (a six-gallon plastic bucket with spigot), five packets of wine yeast, Campden tablets (the sulfur dioxide tablets that are indispensable to the cleanliness and health of wine), rubber tubing, yeast nutrients, a hydrometer, corks, labels, and lots of other things for making other fruit-based wines. We also ordered a carboy, a glass container for the second fermentation. We were too late to order whole grapes—the days have gotten away from us—but we have been able to acquire grape juice: Barbera from California and, surprisingly, Nebbiolo from Italy. Two books were included with the kit, *Winemaking Recipes* and a winemaking primer by an Englishman with an aptitude for chemistry. I'm nervous about the chemistry.

We stash the equipment in the barn and begin to think about making changes to what we'd always planned as a woodworking shop. This space would make quite a nice winemaking room. The barn is naturally cool in summer. There is a porch roof, which would make a nice work-man-like loggia. We can see a tasting table underneath made from the rest of the cedar of the old garage, the porch posts clad in grapevines and roses, small wooden casks inside the barn waiting to be racked. The cogs in the wheels begin to turn.

The juice arrives: a six-gallon bucket of Barbera from Madera, California. We admire the brightly colored picture on its front, which reminds us of the brightly colored Californian agricultural crate labels from the forties and fifties. The Nebbiolo grape juice I've ordered is in transit somewhere between here and Italy. The juice will go into the cool barn, where we hope it will stay cold enough to prevent its fermentation: The batch will be too big for our refrigerator, and we are not quite ready to start the process.

We've bought a backyard vintner's book, all about grape growing and winemaking. We begin to study its pages, cross-referencing to our other two books, and trying to understand about specific gravity, sugar content, and acidity. We learn there's a time to stir and punch down the floating grape skins, and a time to leave the mixture alone. I read over and over the basic directions, trying to memorize their order. I learn about the hydrometer read-ings and how they change depending on the temperature of the unfermented juice, or *must*. The numbers will tell me what to add and when.

This is just a recipe, I tell myself, but it's easy to be convinced that all will be lost if I misread the hydrometer or forget when to add the yeast. Then I think about all the people who've made wine before us, hundreds, thousands of years ago, and how they didn't have hydrometers, and they didn't track time in quite the same way. They fermented the juice, and they let it age, then they drank it, and all was somehow right with the world. Our world cannot be so different.

– 8 –

## wine and wealth and mirth, sing

Others may sing of the wine and the wealth and the mirth . . .

JOHN MANSFIELD

*J* woke with a start from a dream in which I had forgotten to water my grapevines. The bedroom window was open, the night air still pleasantly balmy for August. The wind blew up, wrapping an uncanny whistle about the house. The light was soft gray, predawn, everything still silvered by a setting moon to the west. The night smelled vaguely metallic.

I went outside to check the crate of new vines sitting in a small stone courtyard off the front porch. The vines had been patiently waiting to be planted in the new vineyard for several days now. A spate of rain had flooded the ground over the previous month, but the last few days had been dry, and I had neglected to see if the vine roots, nestled in their humus and packed as carefully as lightbulbs in thin cardboard, were moist enough to survive another couple of days until we'd had time to prepare their new ground. They were dry and the vine leaves had succumbed to the Japanese beetles that slowly feast on my roses in the latter half of every summer, and who begin their gluttony on the day after the Fourth of July as if to mark that day as a national Japanese beetle holiday on calendars. I saw them hiding beneath the vegetation, their shield-like wings, and they had been hard at work making a net-like lace of the young grape leaves. Moonlight shone through this fret-work on my specimens of St. Croix, Marquette, Frontenac, and Frontenac Gris.

I took an old Champagne bucket from the terrace below the house, left out as a reminder of a good party, and filled it with water from the rain barrel beneath the roof gutter spout. I wet the vines until their soil was thoroughly moist. The wind tugged at the hem of my robe and blew my hair in my face. It was probably about three thirty in the morning, though I don't know because I don't look at clocks unless I absolutely must.

Did these grapevines call out to me in my sleep, remind-ing me of their want? It's strange how dreams can hold up a light to illuminate anxiety, how they can point to an overlooked reality, even foretell the future. The August days had been so full, too full, of lists and must-dos that the simple act of caring for my vines had slipped away. I like to think that I responded just in time, and that if I hadn't gotten up in the middle of that night to give them a good long drink, they might not have made it until morn-ing; I might have woken to drooping, brown, and shriv-eled plants.

The same year that I woke from this dream with a start, my husband and I had stood on a piece of land out past my unkempt and best-intentioned perennial garden, out past the small potting-shed-cum-studio, and marked out the rows where we would plant grapes. We had been seized by the notion that this was the right thing to do, plant grapes, as if it made perfect sense, as if it were the obvious choice for our east-facing meadow that we had not yet cultivated in flowers, vegetables, or fruit trees.

We longed to husband the land. No surprise in my husband's case, for he came from a long line of New Hampshire farmers on his mother's side, and we had just learned that on the rather intellectual, lawyerly side of his father's family were farmers hailing from an isolated village in the Vermont hills.

The longing was a little more surprising in my case. The two sides of my family had been made up of educators, writers, lawyers, entrepreneurs. The only known farming in my lineage was perhaps the failed potato farmers from Ireland, potato farming out of not vocation but need, or the Swiss silk farmers who had a grove of mulberry trees outside Neufchâtel. Perhaps I was a true daughter of place, responding to the broad ocean of farmed acreage in the rolling river valley of southern Indiana where I grew up, or to the meticulously cared-for landscape of Italy where I have spent a good portion of my adult life.

In either case, farming the land became an integral part of our work of cooking for our own restaurant, the two inclinations fitting neatly together like pieces of a puzzle.

The first time I ever stood in a vineyard was during my first return to Italy since living there. In the initial few years that were occupied in opening and running our bakery and restaurant, we had not been able to travel abroad. The hours, the money, and the exhaustion would have cost us too much, so we settled for shorter, closer-to-home breaks. The trip that finally took us back to the place that had launched us on the journey of owning a restaurant required months of preparation, reading maps and travel books. We arranged a trip to Piemonte, a region to which we had not yet traveled, and we were thrilled at the twin prospects of going home and going somewhere new. Visiting a vineyard in more than a cursory way was to be at the heart of this particular voyage.

Upon the recommendation of a good friend, who writes very savvy articles about wine and food, we drove to the tiny outcropping of La Morra, not far from the famed towns of Alba and Barolo. We were staying in an old castle that had been converted into a family-run hotel, and we dined at the then-chic restaurant called Il Belvedere, where the view over the undulating hills and vineyards was truly breathtaking. We sat in a clever little wine bar at one of its wooden tables on hard wooden chairs, and we tasted wines of the area with a light lunch. One man, with sweat beading on his brow, ran back and forth between the kitchen and the tables serving and cooking, as well as pouring. We had listened to the nu-jazzy notes of the Euro group playing on the sound system while the patrons around us chatted incessantly about wine. For dessert, we stopped along the way at a bakery and ate for the first time a type of apple cake that seemed scented with roses.

We had called ahead to the vineyard (at least I am hoping we did—and if not I apologize, and now know better). We wanted to see the vineyards and *cantina,* taste some wine, and meet the winemaker. Renato Ratti had been one of the trailblazers in the pantheon of Piemontese winemakers, and since he had passed away recently, we hoped to meet his son.

We arrived at the Ratti vineyard, tucked into the downhill curve of Annunciata. It was a crazy time for everyone there because they were preparing for VinItaly, the big wine fair in Verona. We had unwittingly picked the worst time to visit (outside of interrupting during harvest). Back then, our naïveté was blissful, but now, in retrospect, I can't help but cringe.

In any case, we were treated with great hospitality. We were told to wait for Massimo, Renato Ratti's nephew, who was really the winemaker. Renato's son was the front man, the face of the vineyard, while Massimo worked silently among the vines. As is often the case in Italy, waiting is part of a day's schedule, and it was kindly suggested that we walk out into the vineyard to see the vines until Massimo arrived. He was scheduled to take a group of Belgians on a tour through the little wine museum, housed in an old monastery that was on part of the property. We could tag along with the Belgians if we wished. This was a smart and polite suggestion to get us out of everyone's hair.

We walked out between the vines. This holding was called Marcenasco, a conch-shell-shaped hillside particularly valuable for growing Nebbiolo grapes. A vineyard worker toiled in the distance dressed in blue coveralls and a cap. We walked toward him.

His face was craggy, his nose bulbous. It was a cool afternoon, and he wore a jacket but no gloves. His hands were callused with dirt embedded underneath the nails. He had a sack on the ground next to him and held a sharp-looking yet small knife, almost like the little cutting knife with the orangish-brown handle that Caleb bought at an Italian *mercatino* one spring. (This knife Caleb still carries with him at all times to cut food at an impromptu picnic, or to stop and cut some wild chicory on the side of the road.) The man was grafting vine cuttings onto the rootstocks that had been planted in neatly trimmed rows. It was spring, and the vines were very young, a new planting. He trimmed the rootstocks and vine cuttings, then conjoined them, binding new Nebbiolo shoots onto the older, more established stock that thrived in this soil. It was precisely his action of slicing, bonding, and taping that led us to believe we could do the same thing on our land. We already knew by then that we had wild grapevines growing profusely in the thickets surrounding our meadow. In that moment, we both realized that we could plant this hearty wild stock from home, then graft onto it something more noble.

We left the man to his work and walked up to a rise in the hill that overlooked the vineyard, where we sat for a while watching the landscape unfold. I breathed in deeply of vineyard—a slightly sweet apple blossom smell carried on the air from the neighboring fruit trees, and a ferrous, dusty smell from the freshly worked red earth around the vines. I picked up a handful of the soil and sifted it through my fingers, enjoying the feeling of the arable, living earth on my skin.

There are three images of that day that I carried away with me: the color and fineness of the earth in my hand;

the pruning sheers jutting from Massimo's back pocket that I noticed when we finally met him; and the orange cast to the rim of the Barolo from Marcenasco that we tasted with him and the thirty Belgians after our tour of the little museum. We also carried away three bottles of our preferred vintage. There is still one bottle left in our wine rack in the pantry off our galley kitchen. We wait for the right moment to open it, to share it, drink it, and honor it. I get it into my head that we will wait until we open the first bottle of our first vintage of wine made solely from grapes grown on our own land.

We drive for the first time down the heeled peninsula of Italy's boot. Given that our Vermont winters are so long, we have always been seduced by the promise of sun and heat in southern Italy's springtime. We are not disappointed this year, as the sun shines hot and brilliantly entrancing. The clarity of the light is so sharp and precise that it reflects off the whitewashed buildings and chalk-colored Baroque architecture as if they are made of crystal. Puglia is shaped by its colors: the bright red of the tomatoes; the pristine white of the creamy *burrata* (a cheese similar to *bufala* mozzarella, just *more* so); the clear blue of the ocean; and the green of the fields of wheat stretching for miles. Puglia is one wide, flat plain that reaches from either side of the country to its rocky coastlines. It is also known for its abundance in all things. The farms that populate the countryside are denoted by grand, sprawling houses with walled gardens called *masserie,* the definition of abundance in Italian.

The earth of Puglia is dotted with the biggest olive trees you'll ever see, and its vineyards are obscenely prolific. So much so that, historically, Puglia has been known as a bulk producer of grapes, a maker of cooperative wines. The growers once let these vines produce rampantly, selling off their harvest as blending grapes in thin vintages to noble wine houses in northern Italy and southern France, as well as to cooperatives producing huge quantities of cheap wine.

Cheap and inferior wines defined Puglia for years, until a handful of grower-winemakers decided to change that reputation. More than thirty years ago, families with an inspired vision began to practice the tenets of careful growing, shifting the mission from "more is more" to "less is more." Aggressive pruning became the task. The fewer *grappole,* or bunches of grapes on the vine, the better. They pruned in order to put more energy, nutrient, and flavor into the grapes remaining. Each individual bunch would partake more of the earth: its minerals and water would, in turn, shape the native aspects of these grapes into wine. This significant change in thinking drastically transformed the wines coming out of this region. Men with families and workers like Cosimo Taurino began to rival the winemaking families of the North. Toscana and Piemonte felt the new power of southern wines coming up fast on their heels.

On this trip, it is to Cosimo Taurino's vineyard in Puglia that I want to go. He, too, has passed away recently, but the family is ready and willing to take on visitors. The vineyard holding is located in the town of Guagnano in the

Salento, the flattest and hottest part of Puglia, where the light looks tangible—as if you are gazing at the landscape through an incredibly sheer piece of fabric. We stop in the village for a coffee and we wander the village streets before heading out to the *cantina*.

The village of Guagnano is like a small forgotten jewel and so unlike the Italian towns of the north that have become the clichéd image of Italy. The buildings in Puglia are flat-topped and square with Baroque flourishes, white or brightly colored if the town is wealthy, unpainted and gray stone if the town is not. Guagnano is a combination of the two, a well-cared-for but sleepy little town. The sun is bright at midday, and the town has already shut itself up in order to go home for lunch and get out of the heat. On the main piazza, there is a small coffee bar where we order one of the most perfect coffees we have ever had, the *crema* settling on top of the black liquid, heavy and sweet. The *barista* is the height of modern "glam," wearing a beautifully cut shirt in bright colors worthy of a disco club, his gelled hair arranged in the sharp trend of the day. Incongruously, across the piazza stands a narrow barbershop outfitted in aqua tile with the same aqua vinyl chairs that must have been bought in the early thirties. Manifestos and photographs of Il Duce hang on the walls (*Il Duce* being the sobriquet of the fascist dictator Benito Mussolini). Small Italian towns often surprise in this way; they teeter impossibly on the edge of doing two things at once: moving forward and falling behind.

The Taurino vineyard is not the charming monastery or farmhouse that I have been expecting from my visits to vineyards in the north. It is large and plain—industrial-looking even—and clearly all about the work involved. In contrast with the rather stark lines of the buildings is the warmth of Signora Taurino and her two children, a son and a daughter who help her continue to fulfill her dead husband's dream. They offer us great hospitality by taking us out to lunch at a friend's new restaurant, the only place open for lunch in town that day. Yet they are subdued, their eyes sad, and we know they are still in mourning for husband and father.

Back at the vineyard, Francesco, a longtime vineyard worker, shows us around the *cantina*. We see the maceration machines, the steel tanks, and the small oak *botte* for aging the *riserva* wines. Francesco is trim and tall with a face that could have been drawn by Velasquez, the elongated oval, the brown eyes with the dark smudges beneath, the aquiline nose. He is quite dark, his skin attesting to the fact that he probably spends most of his life out-of-doors. He wears the zipped-up coveralls of the vineyard worker in spring. His flat blue sneakers make him look as if he belongs at the seaside. He drives us in a jeep out into the Taurino estate, where we get out and walk among the vines. The grapes here are grown in the *alberello* style—short, low to the ground like a bush. The trunks of the vines are thick and sinewy. The leaves, large and fan-like, protect the grapes from too much sun and heat later in the season, maintaining a better balance of acidity and sugar. Francesco handles the vines confidently as he explains the art of growing grapes this far south. He motions for me to come and crouch down on the ground with him next to one of the plants. He encourages me to touch the vine on my own. He tells me this vineyard and these particular vines are older than he is.

This is the first time I have actually touched vines. Previously, I have always felt too timid. Somehow to touch seemed impolite. I feared I might do something wrong. I admired growers and vines from afar. But now I reach out. The trunk feels strong, rough, and strangely wise. The leaves feel thick and succulent, like pieces of well-worn oilcloth.

Clouds that come in from the east suddenly darken our wide, flat sky. We stand up and survey the rows and rows of thousands of vines. Francesco talks of vineyard workers' lives: how in the summer months, when it is too hot to work all day, they get up early in the morning, work for a few hours, then break for lunch. They eat in the field, seeking shade from one of the huge olive trees nearby. They eat picnic lunches of bread and cheese, cured meat, small tomatoes, and wine; then they rest during the most brutal part of the day. Later, when the sun has weakened, they work for another few hours. In fall, during the *vendemmia,* the work is constant no matter the weather, until all the grapes have been picked and are in the first stages of crushing. He tells us that the vineyard workers are not rich in money, but they are rich in life. The estate provides not only a livelihood but also yearly benefits of olive oil, durum wheat flour, fruits and vegetables, and, of course, wine. He says, "There is nothing else that we need."

Big fat drops of rain fall intermittently as a warning for the storm that is to come, and we rush into the jeep to get back to the *cantina*. As we drive down the rutted, dirt road, Francesco invites us to join the *vendemmia* whenever we like, and we imagine long days out in the field, the sun beating down, the work hard. We imagine the meditative rhythm of the picking of the fruit, and our grape-stained hands.

The Taurinos have waited for us at the *cantina*, where they have opened several bottles for us to taste. We sample the basic Salice Salentino, a blend of the varietals Negroamaro and Malvasia Nera, and the single-vineyard Negroamaro named Notarpanaro. To finish, we taste the newly bottled sweet wine that was the last gift made by Cosimo Taurino before he passed away, the last vision he had for the vineyard. Cosimo Taurino's son pours this wine into our small glasses with a somber reverence. He tells us that his father thought their land was perfectly suited to growing two non-native grapes, and that they could make a superb *passito*, dessert wine, from these grapes. So they planted hectares of the French Sémillon and the northern Riesling. What he holds is the first wine bottled from that planting. Cosimo Taurino named it Pensiero ("thought" in Italian) because it was the fruit of an idea, a rogue idea, to plant grapes from so far away in this place of lavish heat and sun. It is the fruit of an idea to reform the process and make beautiful, balanced, and elegant *terroir*-driven wines in a place known only for overblown, cooked bottles of rough table wine.

Pensiero's first vintage is fresh and sweet, tasting of almonds. It is light and refined. In one small glass, we taste and pay tribute to the culmination of the pure vision of a man, the fruits of his lifetime. Signora Taurino is smiling sadly and genuinely, the way a widow does when she is remembering the man that she has loved. She nods almost imperceptibly to her son, who presents us with a beautifully carved wooden box holding a bottle of the Pensiero to take home. This will be a most treasured souvenir.

More than five years later, as we prepare the vineyard site for our own grapes, I bring home a bottle of a *riserva* from a particularly good year for Italian wine. It is Taurino's Salice Salentino 2001. We open the bottle for dinner on our night off and drink the wine with a soup made of Tuscan kale, carrots, and beans from our garden. Salice Salentino is relatively light for a wine from Puglia, with a pungent nose of orange peel. Soft, dusty blackberry fruit slides across the palate to finish with coffee and smoke. The wine is stunning and its color shines in the glass against the candlelight, with a hint of orange not unlike that of the Ratti Barolo from the Piemonte that I tasted so long ago.

We are digging holes in the vineyard, getting ready to plant additional vines, and siting more rows. My mind is on my images of the Ratti and Taurino vineyards that I carry, images that have inspired and brought me to this precipice. Growing grapes and making wine seems thrilling—even dangerous. It is a beautiful end-of-summer day, sunny yet cool and windy. I am seized by the memory of my visit to the Taurino estate and the rainy afternoon on which we tasted the first vintage of the Pensiero. I know we still have a little left in the bottle in the pantry that they gave us to bring home, though I can't imagine that it still might be good, for it was opened a very long time ago.

I find the bottle and reach for a small cordial glass. I stand in my own kitchen in my own vineyard worker's attire: jeans, sweater, and Wellingtons. I pour out a small taste, and the wine smells of caramel and pastry. It is still fine, just more pronounced in its attributes after aging in the bottle. The taste is like candied violets crescendoing to bitter almond, with a lengthy, nutty finish.

Recently I have been flagging a bit in my resolve to plant a vineyard, to believe that this is even possible here, or that our wine could be any good. My taste of the Pensiero bolsters me. Cosimo Taurino, a man who went against all the odds, had a vision, which he followed tenaciously. He wanted to elicit the true nature of his native grapes and their landscape. He followed a small fantasy to end out his days—the belief that he could plant and grow two noble whites native elsewhere and bring them successfully together in a small bottle. In this, he beat the odds as well.

I figure my chances are as good as his. If all else fails, I know that there is a tradition of dessert wines in my part of the world. I can concentrate my energy and harness my grapes and the earth in which they bloom into the fruition of my own *pensieri,* my own thoughts.

## — *work, progress: no. eight* —

Our winemaking begins on a Wednesday night. At ten thirty, after a dinner of shrimp cocktail, local cheeses, and various cured meats (called in Italian *salumi*), along with white wine, I am reading by the fire when I decide it's a good time to start the first fermentation. To begin, we must add five to six Campden tablets (the sodium metabisulfite needed to cleanse the juice) and wait for twelve hours before adding any yeast. Between twelve and twenty-four hours later, we can add one packet of yeast, good for six gallons. I figure if we were to start in the morning, we wouldn't be home early enough from the restaurant to get the yeast in on time. On this one point, we agree my plan is sound. Because Caleb and I are both overtired and overworked, we are a little less forgiving that night than we like to think we usually are.

I am not clear on sugar content. By now I've read several passages in several books on this topic, and so many instructions also covered other kinds of fruit and flower wines that I'm a little flustered and not sure if we will actually need the eight pounds of sugar that the diagram says to add to the first fermentation. I do not yet under-stand that sugar is not added to wine grapes as it is with some other fruits. I had never heard that sugar was added to make grape wine, but I think perhaps I have missed some crucial piece of information, some secret between winemakers. There is a lot of "bright" repartee between

Caleb and me about this large amount of sugar, like "But you said we had plenty of sugar," and "You never told me we needed that much sugar." The dialogue sends me into the pantry to hunt down the container, and I discover we do not have eight pounds of sugar. We hope this is not an omen.

Minor panic sets in. We decide to take a reading of the sugar content currently in the Barbera juice at least to see what we need to do; but of course, that leads to yet another discussion, about temperature conversion with the *hydrometer*—a thermometer-like gadget that somehow measures the specific gravity and thus the above-mentioned sugar content in the must, or unfermented juice. We agree the ideal temperature for reading the hydrometer is 59 degrees F. If it is below or above that, subtractions or additions must be made to the reading. Outside it is 50 degrees, a warm evening.

We take a test sample of the juice. Our vial for reading the hydrometer has a leak in it and bleeds all over the dining room table. Again, we hope this is not an omen. We get a reading, and, lucky for us the juice has exactly the right amount of sugar for starting the fermentation process. We are relieved that we don't have to add anything at this juncture, and we can actually get started. We smile at each other and poke each other in the ribs like this was all fun and games from the get-go.

We transfer grape juice from one container to another. The technical term is *racking*. From the large six-gallon container, we siphon the juice with a narrow clear plastic hose into another container that has a spigot near the bottom for easy tasting, and easier racking in the future. The spigot is just high enough on the side of the bucket that the bottom *lees,* or standing yeast, is below the level of the spigot and not at risk of moving with the wine into a new vessel. They say wine should be made during the waxing of the moon, "they" being the ones who know. Tonight there is no moon, no stars, and of course we hope this is not an omen. Five crushed Campden tablets dissolved in a little water get added to our juice, to sanitize the juice and suppress any unwanted activity from wild yeasts or bacteria. Between us we carry the primary fermentation bucket inside and set it in the bathtub like many a good moonshiner before us. First fermentation will happen most successfully at 70 to 75 degrees F, and we know we can keep the upstairs bathroom at that temperature. It's always 70 degrees. We cover the bucket with its clever lid that has a hole in the top for oxygen. Then we place a clean dish towel over the hole to keep out fruit flies.

Now we wait.

# – 9 –

## the green hour

After the first glass, you see things as you wish they were.
After the second, you see things as they are not. Finally
you see things as they really are, which is the most
horrible thing in the world.

OSCAR WILDE ON ABSINTHE

*T*he first time I contemplate tasting that renowned
green liqueur, absinthe, I am a little frightened. My
husband and I are sitting in our restaurant eating our
after-service dinner. The hour is late, eleven o'clock. Our
chartreuse walls surround us, and we must look as if we
are swimming in absinthe, the flickering candlelight cast-
ing watery sparkles and shadows. I have absinthe on the
brain, and not because I have already partaken of too
much wormwood. This is what scares me: the wormwood.
I have heard and read all the horrid stories of debauchery
and addiction, of people falling prey to the Green Fairy,
of the artists' preference for this rumor-laden drink. I
know all about van Gogh cutting his ear off in response
to his absinthe muse, of his drinking absinthe right before
he took his own life. I've read about Manet's first painting of the grim ragpicker, which shows a man drinking
absinthe; and about how Toulouse-Lautrec's nifty cane

flask held absinthe, so that he always had a nip nearby. While I might be intrigued by the Gothic elements of the late-nineteenth-century *absintheuse,* I am more like the stolid 82,450 Swiss who signed the petition to ban the drink back in the early 1900s. The dark tales make the skin shiver, and make me want to be outside on a sunny day drinking something pleasant like sweet tea. Yet I come to the table to taste absinthe because I believe that there is more to this drink than the macabre, hallucinogenic, and dissipated past. I am tired of having been swayed by what I know must be propaganda. I believe absinthe became a scapegoat for a fear that was spreading through a world in an era increasingly defined by uncertainty.

Of course, others before me have been rehabilitating absinthe, and it is already making its long-overdue comeback as an aperitif or after-dinner drink. Slowly, current artisanal makers like T. A. Breaux, the chemist from New Orleans, or Lance Winters, the brewer-turned-distiller from California, have created beautiful jewel-like textures that are now legally labeled and distributed as absinthe. They are craftsmen who became intrigued by the idea of breaking down the historic liqueur into its various parts and reconstructing its recipes.

I must not be like those nineteenth-century women, for I have never before been drawn to absinthe. Perhaps my aversion connects to my alcohol-checkered ancestry. If I were to start down the green road, as it were, would I not be able to return? And yet, I am drawn to wine, to delicate *eaux de vie,* to the hearty aromas of various herbal bitters. Absinthe becomes my challenge. I want to understand this liquid artemisia: to learn how to sidle up to it, become friendly, and banish my fear; and if I go back, follow my own thread out of a labyrinth, I think I may become absinthe's champion.

I travel back to August 1905 when a particularly lurid affair was splashed across Swiss news journals. It is like an evocative ghost story, a real-life ghost story, or the tale of a spirit. The meaning of the word *spirit* here is twofold— voices and faces from The Beyond, but also a spiritous beverage, or liqueur. The etymology of the word *spirit* is curious. Religious men were the first who made alcoholic tonics for the body and for the soul. The potions they created caused a stir in the self. Intoxication was an altered state in which one could manifest visions and hear the voice of God, the Holy *Spirit*. This altered state, at first, was thought to be salubrious.

Yet the men in religious orders were not the first to see alcohol as a means to a higher consciousness. Ancient tribal cultures from all over the world have long made elixirs and herbal concoctions to release human nature from the mundane. It is part of our innate desire as human beings to transcend, to rise above ourselves.

Then there is 1905 in Switzerland. I imagine the scene at the end of a hot August evening, the air hanging thickly, the sky like black velvet, heavy with humidity. Jean Lanfray, a Swiss peasant of French origin, sits in the small two-room house that he shares with his wife, who is pregnant, along with Rose, his four-year-old daughter, and Blanche, his two-year-old baby. He sits at the well-worn wooden dinner table having just finished a plate of sausages and boiled greens, downed with six glasses of wine. There is grease on his stubbled chin, and the room smells salty and fermented, as if someone had recently spilled a jug of red wine on the floor that has turned to vinegar in the heat. He growls at his wife to bring him a coffee. She heats the little pot on the stove, and pours it for him in the small china cup with the chip on the rim, the last remaining china from her own mother that she brought with her when she married Jean. Jean has broken the rest of the cups and saucers. Oh, he doesn't mean to, she reasons, he just gets worked up sometimes. All the men are under a bit of stress. Making ends meet is difficult. She sets the cup gingerly down in front of him. Jean, who never bothers to thank his wife, for anything, takes a sip. It's not how he likes it. He bangs his fist on the table, making the little cup and saucer jump. Both his wife and little Rose (who is peering around the door of the other room watching) flinch. Jean mutters slurred insults to his wife and gets up to walk to the cupboard for his bottle of *marc*, brandy.

The cupboard holds everything of value that they own. Inside are shelves of tin plates, bottles of brandy and absinthe, ceramic jugs of wine. Three baskets contain the cutlery and cooking utensils. Hanging next to the shelves are Jean's old army rifle and a fishing rod. He pours *marc* in his coffee.

This is the end of a long day of drinking, a typical day for Jean. Just today, he had two small glasses of absinthe after breakfast and before work; a crème de menthe, a Cognac, and six glasses of wine to help his lunch down, and another glass of wine before leaving work; a coffee laced with brandy at the local coffee bar on the way home; a liter of wine once he got there; and then that last coffee with *marc* poured into the china cup.

When Jean finishes his corrected coffee, he staggers once more to the cupboard. His wife whimpers a little without thinking, for she knows he will take even more drink, and the drunker he gets the more hell there is to pay. Instead, Jean takes down his old army rifle from the cupboard, turns, and shoots his pregnant wife in the head. Four-year-old Rose comes to the door to see what has happened. When he sees her standing there, he shoots her as well. He steps over his child, his boot in a pool of blood, goes into the little room next door, and shoots the two-year-old Blanche in her crib. Jean then tries to turn the gun on himself but fails, unable to figure out how to point the muzzle at his own temple. As if the horror of his actions begins to dawn upon him, he howls and reels across the courtyard to collapse and fall asleep on the ground, holding baby Blanche's dead body in his arms.

By the next morning, Lanfray was firmly in custody and taken to see the corpses of his wife and children. They were laid out in three different-size coffins, one next to the other. And if Jean Lanfray was not yet sober, this vision might have well done it.

The public outrage over this grisly act was enormous. Despite the fact that Jean Lanfray was a well-known alcoholic, clearly consuming any kind of brew that would keep him well oiled, the locals focused their ire on one detail of the story: the two small glasses of absinthe. Even though

Jean Lanfray had taken his two absinthes early in the morning, hours before the tragedy, and consumed great quantities of other alcohols during the remainder of the day, all the blame was laid on the green, anise liqueur. In just a few weeks' time, 82,450 local people signed a petition to ban absinthe in Switzerland. In the following year, it was.

I travel back to the time before the banning of absinthe, before the starving and dying artists took up its mantle, before the drink got the reputation of liquid opium. Like so many things that end badly, absinthe in its origins showed much promise. In the ancient world, the absinthe plant, *Artemisia absinthium*, with the common name of wormwood, was considered one of the most valuable medicinal herbs grown. An Egyptian papyrus called the Ebers Papyrus (1600 BC) highlights wormwood as a catch-all herb. The writer suggested artemisia as a stimulant and a tonic, an antiseptic, an insect and rodent killer, and a remedy for fevers and menstruation pains. Pythagoras wrote that wormwood leaves steeped in wine ease the pains of childbirth, and Hippocrates also prescribed the herb as a pain reliever during menstruation, as well as for anemia and rheumatism. Galen proposed artemisia for combating fainting spells and muscle weakness, while Pliny, the Roman naturalist, believed wormwood was good for all things associated with the stomach. In the ancient *De Materia Medica,* Dioscorides even considered it a good antidote for drunkenness.

The Renaissance alchemist and physician Paracelsus revived the Egyptian practice of using wormwood to treat fevers, and employed it for malaria. By the seventeenth century, it was used as a treatment for a bizarre cast of ailments: rat and mice bites, poisonous mushrooms, wasp, hornet, or scorpion stings, drunkenness, and syphilis. It freed virgins from "the scab" and cured old men of melancholy.

These practical and useful ways of employing artemisia take out a bit of its stinging modern reputation. In Greek mythology, Apuleius recorded that the absinthe plant was first given to the centaur Chiron by the goddess Artemis, who gave the herb its name. The root of the modern name *absinthe* came from the Greeks as well. They called it *apsinthion* (undrinkable) because of its bitterness.

For a long time, wormwood has been used and proven reliable for treating intestinal worms in both humans and animals. It has also been used (like its relative camphor) to deter moths from destroying fabric in closets and chests of drawers, and even for killing insects.

Even though it made its way in the world based on the good things it could do, wormwood has also long been associated with visionary dreams and with certain kinds of magic. An old wives' tale recounts how a person would see his or her "heart's desire" after drinking a potion of wormwood, vinegar, and honey mixed with other herbs. In the 1858 treatise *Weeds and Wild Flowers,* a certain Lady Wilkinson writes:

> An old belief continues to be connected with the circumstance of dead roots of wormwood being black, and somewhat hard, and remaining for a long

period undecayed beneath the living plant. They are then called 'wormwood coal'; and if placed under a lover's pillow they are believed to produce a dream of the person he loves.

Wormwood is steeped in religious history. There is an account of how wormwood "grew up in the winding track of the serpent as she departed from Paradise." The herb even appears in the book of Revelation after the Seventh Seal has been opened and the bitter star descends from Heaven: "And the name of the star is called Wormwood; and many men died of the waters, because they were made bitter."

The plant called rue is probably the most astringent plant cataloged, but wormwood comes a close second. This is due to its natural chemical compound called *absinthin* ($C_{30}H_{40}O_6$), which has a bitterness detectable even at one part in seventy thousand. The Roman naturalist Pliny wrote that after chariot races, the winner would be given a wormwood drink as a reminder that even victory has a bitter side. This sour, acidic quality has long given wormwood a connection to all things grievous and melancholic.

Records show that modern absinthe appeared somewhere around the end of the eighteenth century, and there are two conflicting stories of its origin. One dates back to 1792 and turns on a Dr. Pierre Ordinaire. A devout monarchist, Dr. Ordinaire fled the terrors of the French Revolution and settled in the village of Couvet just over the border in Switzerland. The story claims that Dr. Ordinaire found wormwood growing wild and rampantly, and prepared his own decoction from the plant. This in turn created the absinthe that has gone on to elicit terrors of a different kind. By the time the doctor died in 1821, his brew had already become known as *La Fée Verte* (the Green Fairy), and was used locally as a tonic. However, another story claims that two sisters from the area, the Henriod sisters, were already making absinthe before Dr. Ordinaire moved into town.

The Henriod story, generally accepted as truth, goes like this: A Major Dubied from Couvet discovered that the Henriods' absinthe cured a number of his ailments: his poor digestion, his tepid appetite, the fevers and chills he sometimes experienced. He was so besotted with the qualities of the Henriods' potion that he bought the recipe from them for a tidy sum and began producing their absinthe on a larger scale himself. In 1797, his daughter married a man named Henri-Louis Pernod, and the two men went into business together. Thus the famous Pernod brand was born.

After some time, Dubied moved the operations out of Switzerland and into France in order to avoid paying an import duty. He and Monsieur Pernod opened an absinthe factory in Pontarlier in the Jura region on the border between France and Switzerland. The drink steadily grew in popularity, and daily production increased from 16 liters, to 408, to 20,000. Other absinthe factories opened all over France and Switzerland, and by the time the drink was banned there were about twenty-five distilleries in Pontarlier alone.

The original absinthe recipes varied dramatically in

style and excellence. The best ones involved distillation, using a grape alcohol as the base; the lesser brands were simply macerated, with vegetable essences added to an industrial high-grade alcohol. A typical recipe required that dried wormwood, also cataloged as *grande absinthe,* along with anise and fennel seeds, be steeped overnight in alcohol. The mixture was then boiled so that the distillate of the alcohol could be paired with the steam-distilled essences and oils from the herbs. To refine and balance the flavors, fresh herbs could be added (such as petite absinthe, hyssop, and lemon balm) after the distiller had filtered the brew. Sometimes distillers double-distilled to increase smoothness in the texture of the drink and also to more fully integrate all the herbal elements and flavors on the tongue.

Recipes and treatments varied from maker to maker, but an important fact to remember is that strong alcohol was not created in the making of absinthe. Absinthe is not like whisky or brandy. Instead, the alcohol, wormwood, and other herbs were simply combined for taste and effect. The traditional green color came from chlorophyll, which is faded by light naturally, and prompted producers to use green glass bottles to protect the color of the contents, these two elements forever associating absinthe with a particular yellowish shade of green.

Absinthe began just as every other liqueur—as a medicinal. Tonics created by the ancients or by the monks in their monasteries took hold as an aid to nourishment—before a meal the drinks whetted the appetite, after the meal the drinks helped digest the food—and absinthe was one of the first of these drinks. It preceded Campari, vermouth, pastis, Lillet, and absinthe's second cousin, which became the altered absinthe recipe created by Major Dubied and Henri-Louis Pernod, no longer containing wormwood, but only anise and fennel, and known simply as Pernod.

I sit in our neighbor's kitchen chatting with mutual friends visiting from California before dinner. A late-summer night in Vermont, the air has already turned cool as darkness comes. We prepare dinner together in unison, one of us slicing tomatoes, another wrapping thin rose-colored prosciutto around fresh figs, and another carefully cutting fresh zucchinis so thinly they look like ribbons of silk. Our friend Michael, the one visiting from the West Coast, is, among other things, a renowned chocolatier. He has brought a sampling of his newest inspiration: tiny bricks of ganache filled with *amaro*. Our cooking and conversation animates the kitchen. First we discuss our favorite *amari*. Then the talk turns to absinthe. I explain to Michael that I have been trying to find a way to confront my resistance to tasting absinthe. He, a true believer, tells me of a good friend of his named Lance, a distiller in California, who makes a many-faceted concoction. Michael himself took a workshop with Lance to learn how to make absinthe; ever since, he has been a convert.

Over dinner, we recount the usual stories about absinthe, ones that I have frankly tired of hearing. As if knowing I am ready to liberate myself, Michael slides right past the clichés. He approaches the liqueur not as a narcotic or stimulant, but as a taste. The nuances of the anise, the subtlety of herbs in the recipe, and the multifaceted layers of flavor are natural subjects for a man obsessed with taste. Like a winemaker, Michael comes to chocolate, to alcohol, or to any food from a completely sensory angle, thinking of its purity and *terroir*.

Michael tells me I must speak with his friend Lance. He predicts I will be lulled by Lance's honeyed voice. Lance, the guru of green, will be able to tell me anything about absinthe that I want to know.

A few days later I am sitting in my restaurant in the afternoon, hours before service, dialing the number for the distiller in California. Lance answers his phone, and like any good ambassador, he is more than willing to talk about absinthe. In my own quest, I want to know what attracted him to it, how he developed his recipe, how he likes to drink his absinthe, how he recommends I take my first taste—for I have yet to savor the liqueur. I sense that I am saving the best for last.

Lance came to distilling as a brewmaster. Beer was his first foray into malts and spirits, but *eau de vie* called to him even more strongly. He worked at St. George Spirits—a craft liqueur company in Northern California started by Jörg Rupf, a German immigrant known as the father of American craft distillation. Lance's interest in absinthe grew from that experience, and he became even more intrigued after reading an article and absinthe recipe published several years ago in *Scientific American*. He began experimenting with making absinthe before he was ever even able to taste the drink made by someone else. As in Europe, absinthe had long been outlawed in the United States, and it was unclear whether a small band of distillers interested in artisanal absinthe would be able to change the United States government's mind.

Reverse archaeology—starting backward from a finished absinthe, re-creating the steps of its creation through taste and research—is what allowed Lance to make the absinthe that he produces now. And today, after much hard work at counter-legislation, the liqueur is once again legally available on the American market. By researching books on the production of alcohol at the time of absinthe's glory days, and by dissecting old recipes found in journals and books on distillation, Lance crafted, over time, St. George's very own Absinthe Verte. He uses the typical ingredients of wormwood, fennel, and anise. Organic wormwood is grown for him in Washington State, and he works with another local farm for fresh herbs as well. He likes to highlight the grassy qualities of the wormwood and support the artemisia with lemon balm and meadowsweet. He adds the mint-clad brightness of opal basil and tarragon to the tonic clarity of stinging nettle. He makes an absinthe, an infusion of herbs in alcohol, quite unlike the Swiss style of absinthe blanche, which is a fully distilled concoction. I like the sound of the words *reverse archaeology*—they point to both science and poetry.

Lance and I talk of the misunderstood *thujone,* that chemical in wormwood often blamed for driving *absintheurs* and *absintheuses* crazy. Thujone appears in very minute doses in absinthe, as it does in other plants like white cedar (often used in home medicinal remedies), tansy, sage, hyssop, anise, and coriander. Thujone, if taken in great quantity, is a convulsant poison. (But almost anything strong, taken in great quantity, can drive you crazy or kill you.)

Most alcohol is a depressant, but absinthe, like tequila, seems to be a stimulant. The chemical makeup of the drink causes the senses to be sharpened rather than dulled. Drinkers of wine or harder alcohols eventually fall asleep. Absinthe drinkers instead talk of a sharpened awareness, or sensation, and emotions that become more intense. The liqueur crystallizes perception.

Lance likes to drink his absinthe neat, after a meal. First he tastes it at room temperature, savoring the combination of flavors. Then he adds a block ice cube (not shaved ice) and allows the magical process of *la louche*. The cold and melting of the ice turns the absinthe cloudy. The cold separates the essential oils from the alcohol, the suspension of these molecules creating the hazy appearance.

I decide that using Lance's method, I will taste absinthe for the first time.

Absinthe's popularity in French culture gained a foothold during the French colonial wars in North Africa, which ran from 1830 to 1847. French troops were given a ration of absinthe to help clean the impurities from their drinking water and as an aid against malaria and other fevers. When the French soldiers returned, they took their taste for absinthe home with them, and military custom soon bled into civilian life. The bourgeoisie quickly picked up the habit. It was considered rather glamorous in the 1860s to be seen on the Parisian boulevards drinking from a green glass. The golden age of absinthe had begun.

During the Second Empire in France, under the reign of Napoleon III, absinthe drinking defined Parisian life. By this time, the bourgeoisie ruled France with great power: Fortunes were made and lost on the capricious stock market. Opera, high-end prostitution, and grand expenditure characterized the Gilded Age. The respectable bourgeois custom of drinking absinthe before dinner became almost universal. The drink increased appetite before a meal, and the hours between five and seven o'clock became known as *l'heure verte,* the green hour. As dusk fell, the air in Paris smelled of anise.

Social custom called for the green drink before the evening meal, a pleasing ritual to end each day and to initiate what the evening hours had to offer. Initially, strict rules of manners prevented absinthe abuse. To ask for an absinthe during a meal, or at any time before or after the proper time, was considered a grave misstep. It just wasn't done.

First, only gentlemen drank it. Then ladies were allowed a glass. As the circle of absinthe widened beyond formal drawing rooms, other converts found an agreeable companion in wormwood: Artists and bohemians took it up. Lastly, the drink reached down to the lower classes.

The bohemian culture's attraction to absinthe seemed largely to rest on the drink's powerful reputation as a vision-making stimulant. In the hands of bohemian culture, the absinthe ritual took on greater meaning and a refinement in preparation, as if the drinker was somehow readying him- or herself for a greater communion with a higher power. The ritual became known as *la louche.* In French, *louche* means "shady, shifty, seedy, dubious." *C'etait une affaire louche:* It was a shady affair. In English, *louche* means "of questionable taste or morality, shady, disreputable."

In order to enact *la louche,* one used a specially perforated spoon made to fit handsomely over an absinthe glass. After 1912, most cafés used the Pontarlier glass, a glass with a bulbous hollow stem that measured perfectly the exact amount of absinthe for the glass. The Pontarlier glass was manufactured after the famous Charles Maire Pernod e Fils poster depicting a still life of absinthe paraphernalia sitting on a table with a Pontarlier newspaper waiting to be read.

With the spoon suspended over the glass, a sugar cube sat on the spoon, and the drinker slowly poured chilled, flat water over the cube until the sugar had completely dissolved. The cold water liberated the essential oils in the herbs used to make absinthe, creating the mysterious and mystical alchemy of clear, green liquid into a milky opalescence. It was believed (and I'm sure is still believed) that the process of *la louche* symbolized the interior transformation of the drinker. Just as the water liberated the oil, the absinthe would liberate the drinker's mind.

It was thought in Belle Epoque bohemian culture that the drink could possibly inspire and lift a starving painter or writer out of obscurity, landing him or her in the Académie Française. However, drinking absinthe could put another person in the asylum, on the streets, or in a coffin. The frisson of holding in a glass the possibilities of greatness and destruction provided a temptation long appealing to the *artiste*.

If the bohemians gave absinthe its dark name, then it was the masses indulging in absinthe that frightened French tradition. The famous phylloxera outbreak of 1859 that destroyed French vineyards drove people to drink other popular libations like absinthe because there was no wine. There is a suspicion, a supposition, that the wine producers saw themselves losing their customers to the green liqueur, and as soon as they were back in the vineyards and in the cellars making wine to sell, they participated in an absinthe smear campaign that was to help remove absinthe from the market equation. Business and sentiment went hand in hand, and absinthe was eventually banned from most places, most countries, most continents.

While absinthe may have had a long setback, the powers who influenced the liqueur's removal could not have taken into consideration the stuff of which absinthe is made. Artemisia is an indigenous herb of remarkable strength and tenacity. Enemies of absinthe greatly underestimated the Greek Goddess of the Hunt. Artemisia would not be eradicated without a fight, and—thanks to distillers like Lance and T. A. Breaux—she has revived.

Late at night at the restaurant, we are sitting at a table for four because there are four of us who've been working; Caleb, his cousin Claire, Victoria from the village, and myself. I can see our reflections in the big Baroque mirror hanging over the banquette, flanked by smaller mirrors of varying sizes hung salon-style. We are eating a dinner of roasted zucchini risotto that tastes slightly smoky and sweet along with a plate of tissue-thin *culatello,* a very refined cured ham similar to prosciutto, and our local Vermont *mozzarella di bufala,* which is creamy and tangy.

After we finish, I bring two bottles of absinthe to the table, both of which I ordered online and received just two days later—a bottle of Lucid and a bottle of Lance's St. George's Absinthe Verte. Two green cat eyes looking out from Lucid's broad-shouldered bottle remind me of a werewolf's or a vampire's stare. But I will not be put off. This absinthe is distilled by T. A. Breaux. I had intended to buy his Jade Absinthe, one of the first modern artisanal absinthes available, but never mind. Lucid is a brand for which he acts as the distiller, and it will have to do. The St. George's bottle looks as if it came straight out of the apothecary shop, large and squat with a red-wax-sealed cork. The label is old-fashioned with a fey monkey cavorting near the script.

We pour the Lucid in our glasses. The first taste will be without embellishment. The black licorice flavor of the Lucid is slightly sweet, and all the herbal elements reflect back at the anise. The sip warms us. No visions. No craziness. So on to the next. I pour and hand the glasses around. Menthol and saddle leather define the St. George's nose. The liqueur itself tastes of a light stroke of anise followed by a finish of tarragon. The basil, the meadowsweet, and the stinging nettle are distinct flavors that call out, then fall into one another like an echo.

We add the ice cubes to our glasses, and the light green drinks turn milky white. Claire, my husband Caleb's cousin who is working with us for the summer, tastes again. She exclaims, "It tastes *mystical!*" I think she's right.

The swirl of the absinthe on the tongue feels exotic and intoxicating in a bright—yes, *lucid*—way. I realize the best way to know something is to experience it. All my reading and research and understanding cannot replace this moment. Pure absinthe makes me forget my fear. Absinthe is simply something to taste, made from green plants harvested from the earth and then distilled in an alembic like a fine perfume. Caleb wears the cologne that I bought for him on the streets of Paris called Fou d'Absinthe (the Craziness of Absinthe), which smells woodsy, mossy, and musky. These elements also flow from the St. George's and grace the tongue.

My mind wanders. I fall prey to my own visions. I see myself traveling forward to next year, harvesting in my garden. I pick grande absinthe artemisia, lemon balm, fennel seeds, wild mint, purple hyssop. I pick the horrid, virile tansy that I cannot get rid of, happy to have finally found a use for the plant. I don heavy gloves and a long-sleeved shirt in order to pick the dead nettle that grows profusely on the property. This will be my special addition to my concoction. I see myself in the barn-garage with a small alembic bought from a woman who sells the petite stills for home use making brandies and perfumes. The contraption sits next to my carboys and small wooden casks of fermenting wine. The vision allows me to be many things at once: I am *une garagiste,* a woman who makes wine in her garage, and I am *maître liquoriste.* I am the would-be *parfumeur.* I am mistress of alchemy.

⌒

## recipe for a pear-absinthe cocktail

I created this cocktail as a challenge from a friend of mine who is an editor at *Cosmopolitan* magazine. Every year, the magazine publishes a roundup of easy cocktails. The ingredients must be simple to procure and store. I imagined that making a drink with a base of Prosecco, or another dry sparkling white wine, would help keep things effortless enough, and since I had recently become enamored of absinthe, I wanted to include it in the drink.

At about the same time, my husband and I had accepted an invitation to spend an overnight at a friend's rustic fishing club not too far from where we live. So I put together a box of possible ingredients and we traveled to the remote club here in the hills in Vermont, very far away from the urbanity of the city. I mixed in the Adirondack-style kitchen, and we tasted my various experiments while sitting on the broad porch looking out over a tranquil fishing lake. Here's the recipe I sent to my friend, and that appeared in the magazine. They called it Pear-fection. I call it the PV3 after the three main ingredients: Prosecco, pears, and—in honor of the original commercial absinthe substitute—Pernod.

- 2 Champagne flutes
- Absinthe: St. George's Absinthe Verte or T. A. Breaux's Jade Absinthe, or in a pinch, Pernod
- Dry Prosecco or other sparkling white wine
- Pear juice
- Fresh pear slices

Coat the interior of one Champagne flute well with about ¼ teaspoon of the absinthe. Pour the excess into the second flute to coat it, too. Discard any excess. Fill half of the flutes with the Prosecco, then top off with the pear juice until almost full. Garnish the glass with a slice of fresh pear, as you would a lemon or orange slice.

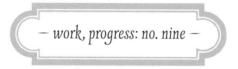

— *work, progress: no. nine* —

Like my anxieties about whether or not I needed to add sugar to my wine, and how to read the hydrometer, malolactic fermentation sneaks up on me when I am least expecting it. I know the basics about how wines are made from my study for serving wine. I know that the juice goes through a first fermentation, then malolactic fermentation. But knowing this intellectually, and needing to know this for making wine, are two entirely different scenarios.

I am reading my winemaking book over, again. I haven't even had this book six months and it is already looking dog-eared and well used. I am learning that while the winemaking process seems very straightforward, there are nuances, or what I perceive to be only nuances, that end up playing a very large role in the outcome of the wine. I am still unsuspecting of these fine distinctions. Take racking, for example. I read in my wine book that *racking* is the wine term for transfering juice or wine from one vessel to another. There is even a very instructive section on how to use a siphon in order to do this efficiently and without too much mess. I read that the purpose of racking is to remove the clear juice from the sediment and yeasts and to introduce a little bit of oxygen into the wine. My wine book tells me that, while racking is important, necessary, and beneficial, too much racking between containers isn't a good thing. (I have another wine book that tells me to rack more often than not . . .) Since racking is oxidative, meaning that wine absorbs oxygen, too much racking can "tire" a wine out.

I think I understand this whole business of racking. But I have failed to pick up the reference to *oxygen*. I have failed to understand that oxygen can be your best friend or your worst enemy in winemaking. Because I have glossed over this nuance, I will learn this lesson the hard way.

That's how malolactic fermentation surprised me. I was reading blithely along, again, about this juncture in the process and not really grasping the importance of monitoring this kind of fermentation. My book plainly states that *malolactic fermentation* (MLF), also referred to as secondary fermentation, does not involve yeast, sugar, or alcohol. It is a bacterial fermentation, which changes the natural, sour-tasting malic acid into a smoother-tasting lactic acid. Not all wines undergo MLF. Usually all reds do, but only a few, select whites.

I take this to mean I don't need to do anything about MLF. I remember reading somewhere that it even occurs quite naturally in red wines. I am too busy fretting about my first fermentation to think twice about MLF. It's only after I think the juice has made it successfully through that first fermentation, and I decide to let it sit for a while before I rack into the next container, that I begin to understand the allure of MLF.

I've been barrel tasting my wines right along. They have a sour green apple nose and taste. Since I've never made wine, I don't know what this means, and don't even know if this is wrong. I ask other friends in the wine trade if they can tell me if this is usual, and they are all as baffled as I am. (None of them are winemakers.) I am on my umpteenth reading of my book when I zero in on the notion that malic acid in wine is a sharp, bracing acidic taste that is not harmonious with the tannins in red wine. In MLF, when malolactic bacteria is added to wine, it consumes the malic acid and converts it to lactic acid and carbon dioxide. MLF eases the palate's perception of acids in the wine. MLF can change the aroma, texture, and mouthfeel of wine. Wines, both red and white, can lose their fresh, green-apple character and develop a rich, buttery quality.

Green-apple quality? Adding malolactic bacteria? What does this mean? Should I have added MLF bacteria to my wine? Did I miss something vital here? Further investigation suggests that malolactic bacteria are often already present in the wine, but sometimes they need a jump start, and that cultured bacteria can be purchased to "innoculate" the wine.

Much like my panic over the question of sugar, I become anxious about malolactic bacteria. I do more research, and everything I read encourages the winemaker to innoculate immediately after first fermentation and before adding any more sulfites for stabilization. It is well after my first fermentation, but I have not yet added more Campden tablets. None of my research really answers my current question, which circles around Time. Is it too late to add MLF? My wine definitely tastes like a Granny Smith apple, and I definitely would like to change that.

I finally send a message to the company out in Missouri where I bought my winemaking equipment, E.C. Kraus. They tell me that I still have time to add MLF as long as I haven't stabilized the wine yet. I order my packets of wine bacteria and impatiently await their arrival.

When the MLF comes, it is the day of the full moon. It's not like yeast that needs to be dissolved in warm water before I add it. The directions say to just add the powder directly, which I do. Nothing particularly interesting happens. No fizzing or big reactions like when I added yeast. I think maybe there should be something more spectacular here, but I feel hopeful that the bacteria will do their work, and I imagine a full-bodied and soft wine.

How blithely and blindly we walk into the future. While I have yet to understand the real nuance of oxygen, I somehow sense that that future holds more frayed and complicated revelations.

– 10 –

*sazerac*

*M*y personal New Orleans has for a long time been one of mythology and imagination. My family once lived in New Orleans, and the childhood stories told to me over dishes of red beans and rice, one of my mother's better recipes, or the King Cakes sent by an old neighbor at Mardi Gras, provided mystery and atmosphere to what I thought at that time was a fairly mundane, quotidian existence. There were foreign spices and Voodoo spells, Catholic mysticism and masked balls, storybook witches and minor tragedies, happiness and brightly colored beads. There were fancy dresses with white gloves and exotic flowers.

I have always felt a particular kinship with the Crescent City. I was conceived in New Orleans, during what I hope was an unfettered moment during Mardi Gras. I also died in New Orleans, which was not happy, and not unfettered, but a product of the unknown and cloaked in ceremony and ritual. My conception and my death? In this case, the two go together, in New Orleans, and yet I am still here to write about it.

When my mother was five months' pregnant, she miscarried while teaching a Sunday school class at St. Catherine of Siena, in Metairie, a town next to and closely aligned with New Orleans. One of my sisters sat in the classroom and saw my mother one minute speaking, the next on the floor in a pool of red. She describes it like one of those slow-motion dreams in which she couldn't quite figure out what was going on, but knew to run and get my father, who was attending Mass. Next, my sister remembers sitting in a Catholic hospital cafeteria. She and my other sister were left there to drink Coca-Colas out of thick plastic straws while our father tried to navigate the labyrinth of doctors, nurses, priests, and unwelcome advice.

My mother tells me that the doctor gave them the bad news: She had lost the placenta. There would be nothing to feed me, I would be stillborn, or even if I lived I would be born severely handicapped at best, and if she took me to term her life would be at risk. Even in 1966, doctors didn't know then what they know now.

Having converted to Catholicism after marrying my father, whose family was Catholic, my mother decided to rely on her own strength and buck the doctors, placing herself in the power of her beliefs. A kindly hospital priest gave her a scapular (one of those little prayer cards encased in plastic and hung on a string to be worn around the neck). It was a picture of the Virgin Mary, and he told her to pray and meditate upon it every day. The doctors told her to keep to her bed. My mother tells me she did both those things, and after an arduous move from New Orleans to another river town in southern Indiana, she was confined to her room during an unbearably hot autumn when the sheets on the bed would never dry and the air felt heavy and oppressive. My mother tells me I was born on

December 8—neither stillborn nor handicapped—born on the Feast of the Virgin Mary's Immaculate Conception and, according to my mother, this miracle is all anyone should ever need to understand the power of faith.

My sister tells another version of the story. All these things are true, my sister says, but what was most compelling for her was the unbidden view of my mother's hospital room in New Orleans after the loss of her placenta. My sister tells me that my mother's bed was surrounded by a circle of nuns in white wimples chanting prayers, and that a priest, his white collar slightly dirty at the starched edge, held the scapular over my mother's pregnant belly and swung it like a pendulum. These two versions of the same experience, true to both my mother and my sister, lead me to believe even more than I already do in the intensity and subjectivity of memory.

This is the first layer of my personal New Orleans. It is like one of those ancient cities that was built and destroyed, built and destroyed, and built yet again, city over city over city—like Cairo or Carthage or Rome or Byblos. This is the bedrock of my story. It happened in a time when everyone indulged in cocktails at lunch and before dinner, so much so that it was no longer an indulgence. A time when pregnant ladies still drank raw milk and ate cured meats. These days, doctors would suspect that my mother had sloughed off an underdeveloped egg. But who knows if what my mother lost was a twin egg? Who knows if this story relates just a random occurrence? I wonder if there is some greater lesson I've missed?

Over the years, I have planned momentous returns to New Orleans, believing that my visit, like that of some prodigal daughter, would fit a large piece of my own puzzle, tell me something more about my family and myself. Over the years, I have had various fantasies detailing my return, and in all of them I am loath to leave, and I imagine setting up a new life there in a brick town house with a wrought-iron balcony overlooking a tropical courtyard, the French doors to which are always open. A ceiling fan just visible on the second floor from the street stirs the air, and a garden in the back is thick with gardenias, oleander, and birds-of-paradise. I have imagined myself a writer there, a milliner, a designer, a maker of absinthe, the owner of a small bistro in a double shotgun building. I have imagined a city in which I eat oysters on a steamboat, or Cajun food in the bayou, or beignets in town. (I marvel at how, in these images, I am always eating.) Each new incarnation of myself gives me another layer of the city, another layer of understanding. It is a cocktail that finally brings me to my conceptual city of New Orleans, and somehow this is fitting.

Other travels have long kept me from making the trip to my own Carthage. There is never enough time each year to get everywhere I want to go. I am surprised I am not a Gemini by birth, as I also have twinned desires: to be both at home and away. The nesting instinct is strong, to set down roots deep into some dark, loamy earth; yet I am almost always thinking of being somewhere else, and, when I go away then return, it takes days, sometimes weeks, for me to unpack my bags. I am sure this has to do with other neuroses as well, my fear of things coming to an end.

The Sazerac. It is a recipe and cookbook that brings me to this cocktail. Hankering for a classic red beans and rice, I pilfer my mother's *Gourmet's Guide to New Orleans* by Caroline Merrick Jones, first published in 1933 with a foreword by Dorothy Dix. My mother's 1960 edition showcases dishes from families-of-good-name as well as restaurant chefs. (Somehow, I am always stealing books from my parents' house—perhaps another neurosis?)

The *Gourmet's Guide to New Orleans* is a gem of a window through which to view New Orleans in a certain era. Picture the ladies' luncheons served on broad screened-in porches, the ceilings painted "haint" blue to keep the hornets confused into thinking they can't build a nest in the sky. The women wear kitten heels and nubbly wool bouclé sheaths with big fat pearls at their necks and white gloves on their hands. As a novelty, they are drinking Russian tea made with oranges, instead of the usual iced tea or coffee with chicory. Old Mrs. Goreau says she doesn't like it quite as well as her *café au lait.* Picture in the restaurants the career waiters in their black tuxedos gliding silently between the tables, plates of plum soufflé and oysters Rockefeller on their hands, or carrying glasses of Ramos gin fizz. Picture the Mardi Gras chaos with late-night suppers on the mezzanines of grand old ballrooms, everyone in masquerade eating *Gateau du Roi* and swirling snifters of Cognac, and searching for the hidden bean or plastic baby inside pieces of a cake made from brioche dough, topped with a sheer icing and candied fruit look-ing exotic and festive. The winner of the game shouts with excitement as she holds up her prize, and takes a kiss on the cheek from the gentleman next to her, who may or may not be her husband.

In *Gourmet's Guide to New Orleans,* there is a whole section on drinks, and I am looking for the classic cock-tail of the city, the one that defines it, identifies it, and the book tells me exactly what I want to know: The drink called the Sazerac is made from rye whiskey, Peychaud bitters, and Herbsaint, or absinthe, that anise-flavored liqueur. Despite not having any of the correct ingredi-ents and nowhere to find them readily in our northern surroundings, I imagine my husband and I mixing the drink and sitting on our couch soaking in the essence of the Crescent. Yet I have spent a good portion of my adult life coming to understand that, to know a dish, and to taste a native drink in its essence and purity, one must go to the source. And so plans for a pilgrimage are finally set in motion. After so many years of imaging a trip south to New Orleans—and having gotten to the stage at which my imaginings have almost preempted my desire to go—what if the city is not what I imagine? What if I am sorely disappointed? But we are talking of New Orleans. What can possibly disappoint?

We arrive in New Orleans at dusk. The sky is darkening, our luggage takes forever to appear on the airport carou-sel, and it takes a while to get the rental car sorted out. It's still hot at sundown, the November air humid. But we

Vermonters relish the slide back into summer. Yesterday was cold and windy at home when I made my husband help me plant the twenty-plus rosebushes that I had let linger in their summer pots for too long. We planted late into the evening, the air smelling of cold metal, planting by the light of flaming garden torches as we raced against the coming frost. After our efforts to get those poor roses' roots buried into the wet, clumpy earth, I am surprised he is speaking to me today.

We drive into the city on Airline Highway, a honky-tonk kind of road with biker bars and strip joints and cocktails-to-go, and wend our way to our relatives' house. I can't quite believe that I am here. I'm a bit numb as we drive around the pretty neighborhood streets, the vernacular architecture embellished by lush gardens, then drive around the derelict pocked and marked roads of the half-abandoned wards with boarded-up houses. I see phrases like 1 DEAD spray-painted on the rotting clapboards. We have come to New Orleans two years post-Katrina, and the ravages of that storm are still ever-present.

The next day, a beautiful, sunny Sunday, I have my first Sazerac. The Café Amelie down in the French Quarter provides a lovely setting. The café is relatively new and not on my list of traditional places to go, like the Napoleon House or Tujaque's or the Carousel Bar at the Monteleone, but there we were hungry and thirsty and I figured, *Why wait?*

Down here, only two years after the fact, one would never guess that Katrina came through, except for the relatively quiet streets in what would normally have been a very busy time of year, the tarmac choked with wild tourists.

The restaurant is tucked back into a courtyard off Royal Street. We eat brunch outside under the shade of a big live oak and market umbrellas. I wasn't planning on having a cocktail for lunch. I had entertained thoughts of Champagne. But here it is on the menu, and I am struck by the idea that I can taste Sazeracs all over the city.

The Café Amelie's Sazerac is a beautiful silky orange color, with the curl of lemon peel like some prehistoric gem caught in amber. It arrives in its short glass that's been chilled, and it pulls in the light like an inverse beacon. Its poetry is offset by the window above our table, the window frame distressed with paint peeling, the window glass dirty, and a torn curtain fluttering at the opening. The drink is at the center of my twin images of this city: the fertile affluence of history and fine living; the shabby dissolution of the Southern Gothic.

The Sazerac beckons with the scent of anise as you raise the glass to your mouth; then there is the remembered smell of horses in the stable eating their sour mash. On the tongue is saddle leather sweetened by rye grain and the taste of molasses even though there is no molasses in this recipe, leavened by the bittersweet of the lemon finishing dry and clean. The effect is sublime.

Some say the Sazerac is the first American cocktail and hails back to the early 1800s. Others might dispute this, but no one disagrees that the Sazerac is one of the first New Orleans cocktails and that it was first invented by a man named Antoine Amadie Peychaud, a Creole apothecary who moved up to New Orleans from the West Indies to open a shop in the bustling French Quarter. He concocted and prescribed a mix of aromatic bitters made from an old family recipe to relieve the ailments of his clients. There is documented evidence that around 1830 he began making a toddy for his friends that consisted of French brandy mixed with his bitters, a splash of water, and a pinch of sugar. According to old-timers' tales, he served his drink in the large end of an eggcup called a *coquetier* in French. (There are romantics who claim that it is the Americanized pronunciation of this word that led to the epithet *cocktail.*)

The Peychaud drink began to show up in local coffee-houses, the innocent name for what were really good old-fashioned bars. One of these houses, a large bar on Exchange Alley owned by a gentleman named Sewell Taylor, was the Sazerac Coffeehouse. In 1853, Mr. Taylor declared that the Peychaud drink would be made only with a particular brand of Cognac called Sazerac-du-Forge et Fils. Mr. Sewell was the sole importer of this fine brandy and had named his bar in honor of it.

Stories tell that the bar was grand enough to employ twelve bartenders, and I can see them all mixing Sazeracs for their patrons, throwing frosty glasses in the air, the glass chilled in a cooler with a block of ice from the icehouse out back, the ice expensive because it had to come down the river on the steamboats from up north.

Soon people in town began to call Mr. Peychaud's drink the Sazerac after the coffeehouse. It is believed that, during this time, one of the bartenders came up with the notion of adding a few drops of absinthe to coat the glass, and, with this refinement, the classic was born.

Around 1870, another gentleman, named Thomas Handy, bought the Sazerac House. He changed the primary ingredient of Cognac to rye whiskey due to changes in American taste as well as the difficulty of obtaining Cognac at the time. Then true absinthe fell by the wayside, banned from all drinking establishments because of the supposedly deleterious effects of its main ingredient wormwood (*Artemisia absinthium*). Where there is a void, however, something will eventually come to fill it, and after the repeal of Prohibition of 1933, the locally produced Pernod-style Herbsaint arrived.

Almost eighty years later—after the ravages of three wars—the bar moved to the Roosevelt Hotel in 1949, becoming the Sazerac Bar and Restaurant. The Roosevelt became the Fairmont, which still stands today, and the hotel pays an annual fee to the Sazerac Company for the use of its name. The company, which produces, imports, and distributes many different liquors, was founded in 1870, by that same Mr. Thomas Handy who bought the coffeehouse and bought the Peychaud family's secret recipe for the bitters.

My second Sazerac comes to my table at the Columns Hotel, where we've gone to listen to late-night jazz. The Columns is an antebellum structure with four white pillars and a second-floor porch, the same hotel where child actress Brooke Shields shocked viewers in the film *Pretty Baby*. There is a banner hanging off the balcony, hailing the return of the St. Charles Street streetcar, twenty-four months after the storm. People sit out in white Victorian iron furniture on the broad veranda eating and drinking and watching pedestrians go by. The live oaks that line the street burst out of their cement sidewalk collars like transforming comic-book heroes popping buttons and ripping sleeves.

We sit in the bar before the first set, which is to be played in the salon, a pretty blue-and-white confection of a room that seems more Scarlett O'Hara than jazz-cat. Here the bar is appropriately dark, with velvet and fringe and college girls drinking too much and flirting with the college-boy bartender.

This Sazerac is a bit of a letdown after Café Amelie's finesse. The bartender uses bourbon, which I learn later is a blasphemy. He doesn't have the Old Overholt, and the anise-flavored liqueur he has on hand is not nuanced like the Herbsaint. The drink is a little too blowsy and tarted-up, reminding me of the phrase *a cheap date*. Even so, the inequities of the drink are tempered by the other elements of the evening, for we are at the Columns and we are listening to the bluesy notes of the banjo and saxophone in the hands of two highly skilled musicians, then to the bourbon-soaked vocals of the man singing about trains, lost love, and hot nights in the rain.

My third Sazerac is like a step through to somewhere else. Our time in New Orleans hasn't been just one pilgrimage to the city herself, but a necklace of little pilgrimages to classic old eateries, to old homesteads that are no longer standing, to old neighborhoods, to dishes tasted long ago, all from a distant family past. My husband keeps having to remind himself as we go to these landmarks belonging to my parents and sisters that I have never been here. Yet these places are so inextricably wound about my own early history that both of us share the strange sensation that we are reliving my childhood memories.

We go to Arnaud's to retrace my parents' steps. This was their favorite restaurant in the city in 1966 when I was born. They've told me about the red bar, the black-and-white-tiled floor, the maître d' who would let them in the alley entrance when they had failed to make a reservation well in advance. They've told me about the jazz musicians who would play at night, and the buttery succulence of the sole amandine and trout meunière.

There is a new bar to the side of the restaurant called French 75, or new since the sixties at any rate. It is rather chic inside with leopard print banquettes, polished dark wood, and crystal chandeliers. We arrive as they open, but—bad luck for us—they are having a private party. We are told we can go to the old bar, and we realize this is where my parents would have sat as they waited for their table. It doesn't look as if much has changed since the midsixties, especially with the menu still hanging over the bar from the World War II era, when you could get an order of lobster thermidor for one dollar. The paint is a bit dull, and the upholstery is worn, but the bartenders are dressed in crisp black jackets with black bow ties. A long, ancient mirror made of cloudy, peeling mercury glass hangs over the bar proper. Old men in coats and ties sit on a wooden bench against the back wall drinking martinis and beer as they wait to go into the dining room. I am sure they have been sitting on this bench since they were young men, rowdy and full of hope. They may even have been here when my parents sat on these same stools. They've been here through the storm—fixtures despite what ails the city. Next to us, a jazz trio gets their instruments ready. One of the young men, the one with the saxophone, is the same we heard just the other night at the Columns. We recognize each other and shout our greetings over the noise of the bar.

The bartender is young but has been at Arnaud's for some time. We ask him to make us Sazeracs and ask, too, if he'll show us his particular dance in the mixing. His southern hospitality is true to form, and he tosses the cold short glass, then rolls it from one hand to the other with a whisper of the Herbsaint coating the inside of the glass, the excess discarded. Then in goes the Old Overholt, a dash of simple syrup, and the long, lazy peel of the lemon, all done in about thirty seconds.

My husband and I sit on the old red leather stools sipping our drinks and watching the crowd. We catch each other's eye in the faded mirror above the bar. We look like people we recognize but don't know, as if we're looking at an old family photograph, yellowed at the edges, of relatives we've never met who lived a long time ago.

There is supposed to be a fourth Sazerac, the one I've been waiting for. The whole trip has hung on a visit to the Sazerac Bar and Grill at the Fairmont Hotel downtown.

I have carefully written down the address from the fancy Web site I found online that tells me I can book a room and reserve a table if I'd like. I've also looked on the city map to see just where it is, so we know where we're going when we set out. I am saving this pilgrimage for the end, like the big bead of the rosary prayer "Our Father Who Art in Heaven" after the ten smaller beads of the Hail Marys. This will be the true test of the Sazerac. The anticipation of our visit is instilled with intrigue and mystery.

We drive down Dauphine Street, looking for street numbers, but can find none. At the corner of Canal and Dauphine is a chain drugstore that has seen better days, and the street itself looks a bit forlorn and wasted. Bourbon Street is just across the way, and there is the tinge of urine and skunked beer in the air. Just one block off the main thoroughfare, the sidewalks are empty, except for the well-dressed maître d' of a tony-looking modern Italian restaurant that's empty and hoping for first customers.

We drive back and forth. No signs for grand hotels. There is one building that looms over the street, a shell of its former self with windows boarded up, and a Baroque marquee that clearly once hung over a broad entrance. One imagines red carpets and gold filigree, but now there is only gray cement and a chain-link fence, and a sign that says DANGER, NO TRESPASSING.

We can't believe we are missing such a venerable hotel, and we circle the blocks thinking we just can't see the entrance. In a frustrated stupor, we stop the car, and I get out to ask the maître d' at the Italian restaurant, who smiles as I approach. When I ask him about how to find the

Fairmont, he confirms the suspicions that have been spinning about us. "Ohhh, I'm sorry," he says. "The Fairmont has been closed since the hurricane. They hope to open sometime soon." He points to the derelict facade across the street, and I wonder if there will ever be a Sazerac Bar again.

Carthage has fallen, and is to be built yet again. Now my true experiences of the city begin to merge with those of fantasy, and the fantasy still morphs in and out of what is real. My husband and I imagine what it would be like to live here. We are somewhat infatuated. We picture a double shotgun house; we live on one side, our restaurant is in the other. In the back, there will be a garden with exotic flowers and roses. Fruits and vegetables will commingle and grow all the time. A pecan tree will be in the corner shading the bed of wild chicory. We will go early in the mornings to the Vietnamese market at the edge of town, and on evenings off we can go for a walk among the live oaks in Audubon Park that survived all that the hurricane had to offer. We'll dine at all the restaurants we've missed on this visit, and dine again at all those we've already tasted. We'll ride our bikes along the levee on the river, admiring its banks. We'll take the ferry out to Algiers and have red beans and rice for lunch on a Monday then drive out to the Jean Lafitte park in the bayou, spooking ourselves with the eerie Spanish moss and sightings of alligators. There will be music at the Columns, though this is not where I'll drink Sazeracs. I'll save that for the little coffeehouses with Old Overholt that play jazz down in the French

Quarter, or for Sunday brunch in the shaded courtyard of Café Amelie, or for drinks and dinner at Arnaud's to pay homage to old haunts. And to show that history goes on, that life goes on, I will drink Sazeracs regularly, though not too much, at the downtown Sazerac Bar when it finally reopens at the Fairmont, come hell or high water.

⤸

### recipe for sazerac

The key to a true Sazerac is in the provenance of the ingredients: the rye, the anise, and the bitters. While many substitutes are available, an authentic drink is made with Old Overholt rye whiskey distilled in Clermont, Kentucky; Herbsaint anise liqueur; and Peychaud's bitters, the last two ingredients hailing from New Orleans. This recipe is adapted from the dry and spicy version prepared for us at Arnaud's in the Crescent City.

1 teaspoon simple syrup
2 ounces Old Overholt rye whiskey
3–4 dashes Peychaud's bitters
¼ teaspoon Herbsaint anise liqueur
Strip of lemon peel

Pack an old-fashioned glass with ice, or chill it in the freezer. In a cocktail shaker, add the simple syrup, whiskey, and bitters. Put a few ice cubes in the shaker, and stir to chill. Discard the ice from the first glass, or take it out of the freezer, and coat the entire inside of this glass with the Herbsaint by rolling the liquid around in the glass. Discard the excess. Strain the whiskey concoction into the Herbsaint-coated glass. Twist the lemon peel over the drink so it catches the citrus oils, then rub the peel around the rim of the glass. Some purists advise you to refrain from dropping the peel in the glass. Others say to add it at the end. I like the way they serve it at Arnaud's, with the peel.

## variation

(adapted from *Gourmet's Guide to New Orleans* circa 1960)

In a cocktail tumbler or old-fashioned glass, moisten one or two lumps of sugar according to taste and crush with a wooden pestle. Add a dash of Angostura bitters and two dashes of Peychaud's bitter and a jigger and a half of rye whiskey. Add two or three lumps of ice and stir with a spoon until chilled. In another tumbler that has been chilled with ice, put one dash of absinthe, twirl the glass, and throw out the excess absinthe. This will give a bouquet to the drink without actually flavoring it. Pour into this glass the mixed drink. Squeeze in a bit of lemon peel about the size of a nickel and put it in the drink, then rub the edge of the glass with a bit of lemon peel and serve. Do not shake or serve any ice in the drink.

## — *work, progress: no. ten* —

Midwinter. We're halfway to spring. The line of days and months in front of us seems long, but the sun has started to shift in the sky, and today it's warm enough that the ice on the road has begun to melt, and the little stream that edges our property has started to run. We while away a Sunday morning reading old garden books and marking on our map the Villa Lante and the Villa Gregoriana, planning field trips when we are again in Italy. We also discuss ordering more apple trees for our orchard and grapevines for our vineyard, to be planted when we return. My thoughts move to the hedge of peony I want to plant, the rose pergola, the hoophouse, the work to be done on the potting shed. We muse about when to schedule the bottling of the new wine. We stop ourselves. It's not yet time to get carried away.

We can taste spring even though we are still eating winter food. We sit down to a Sunday lunch of buckwheat polenta with a pork and pheasant ragu, rich and spicy, followed by a dish of braised radicchio. This is in keeping with the two feet of snow still sparkling on the ground. We think: *Can't we at least do a barrel tasting of our two wines fermenting in the pantry? Can't we get a hint of what's to come?*

There is a fine layer of whitish scum at the top of the Barbera demijohn, but in the wineglass the liquid looks clear and doesn't smell really "off" in any way. In fact, the wine still smells strongly of Granny Smith apples and the palate follows suit, surprising given my addition of malo-lactic bacteria. I try to convince myself that maybe this is typical of an old-style Barbera: light, rustic, meant as an everyday wine, perhaps to be carried in a jug to a picnic in a field. The Nebbiolo, on the other hand, has pretensions. Already, its nose exhibits earth, and on the palate there are fresh violets and a lot of spice at the finish. We think this could be a really good wine.

Soon it will be time to inventory our bottles and prepare them. In May, when it is still cool, but warm enough for us to work easily with the wine outside, we'll siphon our sixty-plus bottles, then let them refine until the end of summer. The end of summer—that molten gold of August, the heavy herbaceous scents in the air, the last hurrah of a heat wave all seem very far away.

We have had our last night of the winter season at the restaurant. We have filed our paperwork, cleaned out the refrigerators, left an "away" message on the answering machine, and locked the doors. At home, we finish pack-ing, clean the house, and generally try to organize our lives so that we can be away for a month and not feel our own absence too much.

Twenty-four hours before we fly out of Boston for Milan, I decide I should do another barrel tasting of our wines, patiently waiting in demijohns in our pantry. The fine layer of scum that has accumulated on the top of both varietals has been giving me some good pause. As well as tasting, I think perhaps I should look at one of our wine books and try to determine what is actually causing said scum. If it's natural, I'll have nothing to worry about.

It turns out that I have done two bad things: I have left the wine sitting on dead yeast cells (the lees, or bottom sediment) for too long, and I have exposed the wine to air without racking, or transferring it to another vessel and resealing it until the next racking or the bottling. The combination of air and dead yeast has made something ugly with a very pretty name: *flowers of wine.* A bacteria is making little white flowers or flecks on top of the juice. When there are just dots of white, it is possible to save the wine, but when the dots merge to become a thick layer, it is too late. I think it is in fact too late for the Barbera, but there still may be hope for the Nebbiolo. We decide to follow the directions for correcting this condition for both wines and see what happens.

My wine books don't tell much of what *not* to do. They explain how to measure sugar, how to rack, how to sterilize equipment, but they don't talk about the mistakes of first-time winemakers. There is nothing about how best to facilitate a barrel tasting, and nothing about when to rack if you want to let your wine sit longer in the carboys before bottling. It is as if they take it for granted that these things will be obvious to you.

So we rack the two wines, straining as we go along, and add the requisite Campden tablets (one for each gallon), the sulfurous sanitizer. The Nebbiolo goes into a bucket with an air-lock spigot—for barrel-tasting safety—and the Barbera into another carboy (we only have the one bucket with spigot). We hope that all goes well over the next month, and we'll know if this solution has worked just by looking at the Barbera in its glass jar when we return. Fingers crossed.

While we'll be disappointed if our wine isn't drinkable this vintage, the lessons I've learned have already been great. I could have read those wine books backward and forward, and the necessities of how to handle the wines would never have made real sense to me without my making the mistakes that explain the reasons behind the steps of the winemaking process. We must fall before we can rise.

*– 11 –*

*little water*

$\mathcal{I}$n a cold November, more than ten years after the Berlin Wall came down, Caleb and I arrived in the city of Minsk for the first time. We had to show hard-won visas and letters of introduction at the kiosk before they would let us through the secured gate. There had not been many people on our flight from Germany, so it didn't take us long to pick out our luggage. Laden with our bags, we spotted Olga at the entrance to the gate. She was standing next to her father, Slava, whom we had only seen in photographs. Raisa, her mother, was not able to come to the airport as she was at work, but would meet us later. We smiled, and waved, and felt like crying.

By that time, Olga and her sister Tatiana had worked with us at the restaurant for several years. Olga had first come to the United States from Minsk one summer on the Fourth of July, armed with a five-month work visa. By accident, she showed up at the door of our restaurant looking for work; she even came to our town by accident. Both were happy accidents, and Olga decided to stay and complete her studies in America. Her sister, who came the next year, made the same decision.

We, too, had once been like them, foreigners in a foreign land, deciding to make a life far away from what had once been home. We recalled how for us, the idea of home began to change, one home replacing another, as first language gave way to a second. These things we understood. With Olga and Tatiana we shared this experience even as we shared hours of work together at the restaurant. We shared holidays, and arguments, occasional sadness, and much laughter. We became an intentional family, choosing each other for both obvious and private reasons.

Now Caleb and I were traveling to Minsk to meet Olga and Tatiana's parents, to extend our notion of family, and to learn more of their Belarussian culture and language. Unlike the first words I had learned in Italian, my first word in Russian—learned months before taking our journey, and learned out of the desire to communicate during work in this other language—was the one word *vada*, water. The second word I learned was *vodka*, little water.

My own history with vodka starts long before my meeting Olga and Tatiana, and long before my husband and I even thought of traveling to Eastern Europe. I learned to drink vodka in college. I hadn't developed a taste for beer yet, and I'd had a bad experience with a gallon jug of Ernest and Julio Gallo's Hearty Burgundy so I would not become interested in wine for a few years. My parents' inclination for Irish whisky had not lured me—my dislike of it decided when I was young and asked to take a sip from my father's cocktail glass. It was strong and bittersweet, not to be my tipple of choice. I must have first tried vodka at one of those college parties where most people drink beer, and where bad vodka and cheap bourbon are served for those who don't like Heineken, Rolling Rock, or Budweiser. My first experience of vodka didn't leave an impression other than my liking the clean taste; and the liquor didn't seem to leave me addled or incoherent.

Vodka became my drink of choice, and it was the drink I could down quickly and easily in a small shot glass and beat any drinking-game opponent without difficulty. I liked it even better when I could have it at a bar, doctored with sweet tastes like Kahlúa and cream. My preferred college cocktail was a white Russian. Who knew that someday I would board an airplane for a country where I had connections, a country named Belarus, which means "white Russia" in translation.

My fascination with vodka eased into other interests— wine, beer, and brandies—but a vodka tonic was my summer drink, the lime adding just the right amount of fruit. In fact, in my recollection, the only cocktails I drank were vodka-based: a madras with cranberry and orange juice; a Cape Cod with just the cranberry and a lime; a salty dog with white grapefruit. When I got much older I graduated to the vodka martini because I loved green olives, and to the vodka negroni because I loved Campari. I've never been a fan of the other clear liquor—gin.

Before arriving in Minsk I knew enough to know that Slavic cultures prized their vodka, and that vodka was often the bane of the depressed Slavs. They drank it in the morning, they drank it with lunch, they toasted with it, and they drank it with dinner. They drank it like water— their little water—a *lot* of little water.

The drive from the airport to the city of Minsk was colored gray, brown, and dark green. Forests of pine trees and naked poplars lined the highway. A cemetery thickly populated with both headstones and fir trees went on for what seemed like miles. Heavy branches extended overhead. While off in the distance, in the waning, cloudy light of the afternoon, we could see settlements of *dachas,* sweet little country cottages with vernacular flourishes like bright paint colors and gingerbread trims, making a valiant contrast against the bleak beauty of the landscape. Almost all citizens of Belarus have their own *dachas,* a holdover from the Communist regime during which all citizens had a right to a piece of property in the country on which they could grow fruits and vegetables to carry them through the winter. Even now, the citizens can't own their property—all land is owned by the state—but have it on a life-long loan.

Slava drove his new car, a Volkswagen, which his daughters had insisted he buy. In their opinion, his former car was so old as not to be safe or trustworthy. He didn't particularly like this new car, which by American standards would be considered aged. A strong used-car market thrives in Minsk, and very few people drive a new car straight off the factory floor. Slava preferred his old car, a Lata, that classic Eastern European vehicle, which he had bought in the early seventies and had kept running ever since. Slava is an engineer and has a garage not far from their apartment in which he can spend hours tinkering and tuning up.

That November, Minsk was a city experiencing a renaissance. The sly President Lukashenko had begun a campaign for renovating civic buildings, cleaning up public parks, and generally sprucing things up. The result was a sparkling city with an impeccably clean subway system where young people on dates spent hours sitting on benches and talking. There was a manicured city park enhanced by a lake and statues of great Russian figures. The historic district was getting new paint and new windows. The department stores were full of clothing in the latest fashions, shoes, and china. The food markets brimmed with fresh breads, cured meats and fishes, prepared foods, and fresh vegetables.

Restaurant culture had taken off, with new Italian, Mexican, and even Japanese eateries drawing crowds of young people. In the few years that Olga had been gone, dining out in Minsk had become a pastime. Before, she couldn't remember there being any restaurants except for one or two fancy Belarussian places where you went for wedding receptions and other special occasions. Now pastry shops and chocolate shops opened their doors, and students stood at counters eating little tea sandwiches and cream puffs with cups of hot fruit infusions to wash it all down. Even the fast-food restaurant in the city center, called Maxi-B's, thrived. The spot put our own notions of fast food to shame. The decor was modern and very clean with a battalion of employees bussing tables and wiping them down, preparing them for the next customers. The food offered was cafeteria-style, but house-made, and we ate delicious borscht and sausages one day for lunch. Not only young people frequented Maxi-B's. We sat next to an older woman treating herself to a long lunch out dressed in her finest coat.

Everyone walked everywhere. People looked happy. The women were beautiful, willowy, and well dressed. Clever Lukashenko, giving the people enough freedoms and enough money that they shopped, they dined out, they went to dance clubs. Black-market economies grew. A bright little capitalist culture emerged out of the dreary Communist period. He had given the people something to lose, and therefore solidified his own political longevity.

Behind the prosperity, the government lurked, and everyone knew it. One had to be careful of what one said, or where one was seen, or what one was seen doing. Visas were required for both entering and leaving the country. It was still very difficult for anyone to get visas to travel elsewhere. And the Belarussians, both government and people, were very suspicious of Americans. Olga warned us about us about speaking English; she was afraid the use of our own language might cause trouble, even though we had all the proper documentation to be there visiting.

Slava and Raisa's apartment was near the park. The residential buildings in Minsk, classic Soviet-style mono-liths, tower over the streets. From the outside, they look in need of much repair. Flaking paint, crumbling exteriors, and dank, open-to-the-air lobbies that smell of urine and vinegar. The no-frills elevator clicks along, but sometimes breaks and stops midway and you are stuck.

Once inside the apartment, however, warmth and brightness enveloped us. From the derelict hallway with elevator, we passed through a rather chic vestibule belong-ing to Slava and Raisa. All the locks were opened with what looked like a jangling set of castle keys. We entered the front hall, lined with cozy fur coats and beautiful leather boots. The whole apartment was stylish with intriguing brocade wallpapers, a newly installed kitchen and bathroom, three bedrooms, a living room, and two balconies. The environment was lush and homey at the same time.

We ate a lunch pre-prepared by Raisa of chicken broth with little veal meatballs, cured salamis, a carrot salad, and cookies, fresh fruit, and tea to finish. Olga translated all our many questions since our Russian comprised only a few words. I carried a little black notebook in which I constantly wrote, trying to figure out the new alphabet and the meaning of the letters. Slava had no English. Caleb drank *piva,* beer, then we had only a few minutes to organize ourselves before meeting Raisa after her work at one of the many government offices. There we would need to sign in again and make our presence officially known.

Meeting Raisa for the first time was rather astonishing. She was one of the most beautiful women we had ever seen. Her heart-shaped face had cat-like eyes and creamy skin that was marked by much smiling and laughter. She gracefully ushered us through the obstacle course provided by the bureaucratic foreign office, and signed her name on a dotted line, taking responsibility for all our actions while we stayed in Belarus. The office was antiquated, lined with filing cabinet after filing cabinet, each not quite closing because the drawers were so full. At the desks sat tired-looking office workers. Olga told us that nothing was on computer; all their files were still paper. Then, as if the bureaucrats might think twice about our sojourn in Minsk if we stayed in the government rooms any longer, Raisa, Slava, and Olga hustled us outside. Next thing we knew we were back in the car, and driving to the Belarussian National Ballet.

All this while, we were looking for vodka. Olga had cautioned us about the vodka traditions here in Minsk. The long parties where rituals of philosophical and rather literary toasts with small drinks of vodka after each speech. We had been too busy to sit down for toasts at this juncture in the trip, occupied as we were with arriving, eating, signing in, then viewing an awe-inspiring rendition of *Giselle* at the ballet. At intermission, we ate little smoked salmon and caviar sandwiches with Champagne, and tried to keep our eyes open through the second half of the story. A brilliant finale with sparkling lights and effortlessly flying ballerinas kept us awake.

The vodka would come later. Slava and Raisa did not drink much normally, occasionally a beer or glass of sweet wine with dinner. At that time, Olga and Tatiana never liked drinking, either, even in the States. Drinking seemed to make them uncomfortable if someone began to have too much. The dangers of an alcoholic culture (always seeming to hover at the edges) were never far away.

One evening, Olga wanted to host a party to introduce us to her friends. Raisa spent two days cooking a banquet of hors d'oeuvres: a variety of Russian salads, toasts with spreads or smoked fishes, caviar blinis, plates of cured meats, Russian eggs, cherry tomatoes stuffed with garlic, cheese, and mayonnaise. She also prepared a delicious main course of veal stuffed with dried currants. There was wine from Moldavia, and beer. But most important was the Belarussian vodka with its white-and-green label of the prairie bison. The vodka itself is slightly discolored, and floating in the bottle is a single strand of bison grass, a traditional Belarussian flavoring, with the grass imparting some of its color.

We were eight round a big makeshift table in the living room, the table dressed with an intricate lace tablecloth. Raisa and Slava presided while Olga entertained us all. Olga, her parents, Caleb, and I welcomed Olga's friends: Skusha, Sasha, and Katya. Sasha, originally from Ukraine and married to Skusha, spoke excellent English. He and Olga translated. There were comparative conversations about the United States and Belarus. When talk veered toward politics, Olga steered it back to off-color jokes. It is always difficult to manage a dinner party when half the people cannot directly speak to one another, but Olga and Sasha guided us all as best they could.

Slava began the toasts. Raisa poured the vodka into our petite glasses. Slava's toast followed precedent and was long, philosophical, and very affectionate. All of us assembled clinked our glasses for the first time that evening, and each took a sip. Sasha and Slava were well practiced and downed the glass. I savored the taste, which was redolent of cinnamon as well as the spicy flavor imparted by the bison grass.

We toasted on into the night, Russian pop music playing in the background. I recall that we pushed back the table and danced, but this may be something I imagined, knowing as I do that all Belarussian parties devolve into dancing, eating, and drinking vodka. In any case, I have a very fond memory of that evening's food and drink shared with friends and family. We were brought together by the delicious tastes made by Raisa, the eloquent words of her husband, and the gossamer flavors of Belarussian vodka.

The first documentation of vodka in Russia was at the end of the ninth century. The first known distillery sprang up at Khylnovsk, recorded about two hundred years later. Poland and Russia have often argued over who first created vodka, and Poland lays claims to having distilled vodka as early as the eighth century. However, Polish records show that, since these first vodkas were a distillation of wine, they might be better defined as crude brandy. The first real Polish vodkas appeared in the eleventh century when they were called *gorzalka;* and, as with every alcohol, they were originally used as medicines. During the Middle Ages, vodka was used not only for medicinal purposes, but also as an ingredient in gunpowder. In the fourteenth century a British ambassador to Moscow first described vodka as "the Russian national drink," and by the mid–sixteenth century it was established as the national drink in Poland and Finland as well.

Vodka consists of water mostly and ethanol purified by distillation. Often the ethanol, made from fermenting potatoes, grain (usually rye or wheat), or sugar beet molasses, undergoes multiple distillations to refine it. Even so, there can also be traces of flavorings or unintended impurities left over from the distillation process. In the past, in order to mask the impurities and rough taste, distillers flavored their spirits with fruit, herbs, and spices.

Centuries ago, Russia produced several kinds of vodka (or *hot wine* as it was called). The Russians made three grades of vodka: *plain wine, good wine,* and the highest quality available, *boyar wine.*

By the middle of the fifteenth century, pot distillation in Russia had made an appearance, most likely an influence from Turks with whom Russia had constant power struggles. Before the arrival of pot distillation, or the alembic still, the processes of seasoning, aging, and freezing were all used, but freezing concentrated the impurities of the alcohol. The chemical procedure of *precipitation* using milk, egg whites, or isinglass from the air bladders of sturgeons was developed to help clarify the liquid.

Around 1450, vodka started to be produced in large quantities. The first recorded exports of Russian vodka went to Sweden in 1505. Polish *woda* exports started a century later from major production centers in Posnan and Krakow. Three hundred years later, owning distilleries in Russia became the exclusive right of the nobility. The nobles, each wanting to produce a better or more intriguing product or to hide a multitude of sins in the alcohol itself, began to infuse vodka with aromas and essences. Since there was no standardized process for making vodka, distillers could be as winsome as they desired. Vodkas with particular flavorings appeared in the glasses of the rich and on tsarist tables. Heady essences laced the strong liqueur: absinthe, acorn, anisette, birch, calamus root, calendula, cherry, chicory, dill, ginger, hazelnut, horseradish, juniper, lemon, mastic, mint, mountain ash, oak, pepper, peppermint, raspberry, sage, sorrel, wort, and watermelon.

Typical of the production process in the time of the tsars was to distill the alcohol twice, then dilute it with milk and distill it again, adding water to bring it to the required strength and then flavoring the vodka, prior to a fourth and final distillation. Felt or river sand was often used for filtering out unwanted particles. Vodka was not at that time inexpensive to make, and it remained largely a craft production. In the eighteenth century, a professor in St. Petersburg discovered a method of purifying alcohol using charcoal filtration.

In combination with the refinement of the distillation process, the Napoleonic Wars increased the popularity of vodka. Russian soldiers trying to survive in the cold, brutal war zones of Europe began to rely heavily on the spirit for emotional as well as physical support. The demand for vodka increased exponentially, and cheaper, lower-grade vodkas made from distilled potato mash began to appear on the market in order to fill the need. By the end of the 19th century, with all state distilleries adopting a standard production technique, the name *vodka* was officially and formally acknowledged.

After the Russian Revolution, the Bolsheviks confiscated all private distilleries in Moscow. A law was finally enacted in 1894 to make the production and distribution of vodka in all Russia a state monopoly. The government saw the financial gains to be made. Those in power also saw the broad epidemic of drunkenness affecting their people given the availability of the cheap, mass-produced vodkas, both imported and home-produced. The state could get rich while at the same time monitoring the nation's intake.

As a result of the revolution, a number of Russian vodka makers emigrated, taking their skills and recipes with them. One such exile revived his brand in Paris, using the French version of his family name, Smirnoff. Monsieur Smirnoff, with another Russian émigré from the United States, formed an alliance and set up the first vodka distillery in America in 1934. This distillery was subsequently sold to a US drinks company. By the 1940s, vodka had become commonplace throughout the Western world.

There is a man here in Vermont who makes vodka. Duncan and his wife, Ping, settled a piece of wild land in the region known as the Northeast Kingdom. He bought an old farm with only the cellar hole of a barn left to claim that the acreage had once been inhabited. They came to Vermont from Singapore, where they both taught at a university. Duncan had been an anthropologist studying mountain cultures, how people made a living in the hills. After all that research, he decided he wanted to reside more fully in a mountain culture, and once they had found their property tucked into the green hills, the question became how to live on and from their land.

Duncan is a chemist by nature, so distillation was a natural attraction. He discovered that he could make vodka from maple sap—fortunate given the thick sugarbush on their hillside. Building his own still, he developed a unique style of vodka making. The liquor found its way to somebody who knew somebody who knew somebody. His creation won acclaim and garnered attention on a grand scale very quickly. Soon he was making a living making maple vodka, and his own sugarbush was not enough to feed the demand. So he produced a vintage vodka from his sugarbush, and made a vodka christened Gold from a nearby maple farm. He had figured out how to live in the mountains.

A few years later, Duncan and Ping watched a film called *Genghis Blues*, in which a blind musician in San Francisco decides to teach himself to become a Tuvan throat singer just by listening. The story involves a trip to the outer reaches of Russia, where a performance is toasted with glasses of Tuvan milk vodka. Duncan immediately thought of all the cow's milk available in Vermont. He learned that Tuvan milk vodka is actually made from mare's milk and is frozen post-fermentation to concentrate it, so it is not a true distillation. Duncan took cow's-milk sugars from a local dairy and began his own experimentation.

Despite being somewhat of a mad inventor, Duncan does not look as if he has just put his finger in an electric socket. He wears a trim beard and haircut, both flecked with gray, and is dressed simply like any other Vermont farmer. In conversation he always reaches for the next idea, or is able to discuss the alchemical magic of his distillery like a poet. He uses evocative words like *erasure, curve, esters, heads,* and *tails.*

Standing in the distillery on a sky-blue summer day, he talks to me passionately about how poorly most vodka is made. He speaks with depth about the process of distillation and the difference between the mass producer and the artisan. Having almost failed chemistry in high school, I work to keep up.

Duncan describes how vodka is made in volume in stainless-steel tanks, and is often rife with impurities, so the distillers must filter and strip the alcohol of everything— what you taste when you sample these vodkas is *erasure*. He likens this to a blank canvas that the painter prepares with a coating of gesso, but then, strangely, the painter removes all the gesso from the canvas, and then the stripped canvas becomes the "painting". If, like the erased canvas, the distilled vodka is not actually stripped in the filtering process, then the alcohol is masked, as reflected by the popularity of all the flavored vodkas currently in vogue that have an additional flavor added at the end of the process.

Naturally, vodka will be riddled with impurities. At 190 proof, the liquid will host a variety of expected chemicals: methyl alcohol, acetone, ethanol. Some are good; some are bad. Ethanol resides in the center of the alcohol "spectrum" with other chemical compounds at the top and bottom or, as they are called by the distiller, the heads and tails. *Heads* are made of lighter compounds and give liquor that "lighter fluid" element of taste; *tails* include heavier compounds. Both can be poisonous, but *esters,* a range of microscopic flavoring elements natural to the alcohol, can reside close to the heads or tails. Raw alcohol and acid make up the compounds of the esters, a combination that gives liquor a "fruity" quality. The challenge for the craft distiller is to find out where the flavor esters exist, then to distill to that layer in order to create

a nuanced and refined alcohol. When distilling something like maple sap, the flavor esters lie nearer the heads.
Distilled alcohols that have a smokiness or saddle leather
quality in the nose and on the palate reap the benefits of
distilling closer to the top.

Duncan uses a type of fractionating still, mostly
amended by his own experimentation and inventions.
A *fractionating still* settles out the various compounds
and layers of the substance being distilled, so that the
distiller can more easily remove the unwanted elements.
Distillation becomes a constant process of tasting and
amending, a full circle of creation. In Duncan's opera-
tion, in the purest holistic sense, the sap comes from the
trees on the land, and the wood to fire the boiler from the
still comes from the trees on the land, and further distillation processes are literally fueled by the unwanted chemical compounds fractionated out of the vodka.

We taste his morning's distillate of maple vodka. We
taste in wineglasses because Duncan thinks the bowl of
the glass increases the headiness of the perfume. This is
the key to understanding the curve of vodka's flavor and
scents, just as in wine. The vodka shows incredible structure in the glass with ropes of liquid streaking down the
sides of the glass. I smell a wet, snowy, winter mountain
stream and wood smoke. On the palate, Duncan's maple
vodka is also smoky and slightly caramelized. He is pleased
with the tones developing in the process.

Next we taste the 2005 Vintage Maple from his own land.
The vodka shows fruit right at the front of the nose and

the flavor arc. The center of the taste is clean and quiet, and the finish tastes of butter and nutmeg.

Duncan pours his new plum vodka in our glasses. At a recent launch party in Washington, DC, he met a farmer from the San Joachin Valley in California, where most of California's fruit farms are situated. This farmer bemoaned the loss of portions of his plum crop because the fruit had either too many small blemishes or not a long enough shelf life to go to market. He didn't like the waste created from the rejection of perfectly useful fruit. He and Duncan hatched a plan to produce a plum vodka together that would use the leftover plums. Duncan hopes to craft a very refined, fruity vodka. Already, his vodka exhibits the essence of plum.

We do not need to taste his milk vodkas because I am already familiar with his White. Duncan's milk vodka is creamy and incredibly smooth, and the sweetness of the milk comes through in the nose as well. I look at the bottles of it lined up in his tasting area, strong broad-shouldered clear glass with lightly etched floating maple leaves, or the pale outline of a cow in the label. On the White bottle, Duncan recommends drinking the vodka straight or in a white Russian. For just a few seconds while standing in his distillery, I am thrown back to my own early history with vodka and those easy-drinking college cocktails over ice. Then, for a few seconds, I am back in Minsk sitting at a table covered in white lace. In a perfect, amended memory, Olga and Tatiana are both there, along with their parents Slava and Raisa. The music is loud and the dancing has just begun.

⤳

### recipe for classic white russian

This is the traditional white Russian recipe I remember. As with anything, the ingredients are key, and I recommend using a vodka made from milk sugars and that is very creamy in texture like the Vermont Vodka White made by Duncan. The resulting drink could be a nice liquid dessert.

- 2 ounces Vermont Vodka White, or other vodka
- 1 ounce Kahlúa, Tia Maria, or other coffee liqueur
- Light cream

Pour the vodka and coffee liqueur over ice cubes in an old-fashioned glass. Fill with light cream and serve.

⤳

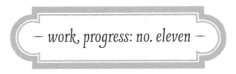

*— work, progress: no. eleven —*

The weather here in Vermont shifts back and forth between hot and humid, and rainy and wet. The hurricanes traveling across the ocean, whirling dervishes of wind and disturbance that are spawned in Africa and take aim at the Caribbean islands and Gulf Coast, always threatening coastal Texas and New Orleans. Here in Vermont, we tend to get the remains of the extravagant winds and rain, bringing tempestuous unpredictability to our northern reaches.

These wild days remind me that I need to bottle my wine. The end of the season is fast approaching, and I think my fledgling wine has had plenty of time to sit and stew. It's probably a good idea to get it transferred into glass bottles so it can settle and relax in the wine rack next to the wood rack in our barn-garage before the cold frost blankets the ground. Frost, that net of shimmering white crystals, so pretty in harvest moonlight, in the brightness of the next day is revealed as a cruel trickery. It leaves a trail of blackened stalks and vegetation.

I have collected used wine bottles from the restaurant and they sit in boxes waiting to be washed and sterilized, their old labels waiting to be removed. Here are the remains of good wines—bottles emptied of Aglianico from Campania, Ciró from Calabria, Primitivo from Puglia, and Nebbiolo Langhe from the Piemonte. Here's sturdy dark glass from an old-style Chianti producer. I want my wine to be cloaked in respectable, heavy glass. Even though it's a small wine, I hope it will rise to the challenge of a good vessel.

On a sunny day, I set up the galvanized metal washtub with water warmed from sitting in the hose. The cases of used bottles get filled with water themselves then packed into the tub, the water inside keeping them from bobbing up. I'm looking for the minimum of work here, imagining the old labels gently sloughed off the glass on their own.

There is no such luck. Some labels are adhered with

an industrial substance that is "tighter than two coats of paint," as they say in these parts. When I think the bottles have had enough time to soak, I see that my job will not be so easy. I must scrub and pick and scrape to get some of these labels off, and still the glue sticks and makes the bottles look pocked and dirty. I start over. I soak the bottles in *really hot* water in the sink in the kitchen. This works a bit better.

Since I have lost all our Barbera wine to my naïveté, there is only the Nebbiolo to bottle, and that is cleverly contained in the bucket with the spigot. I soak the bottles once again along with the clear plastic siphoning tube that came with my winemaking kit, all in a sterilized solution in the kitchen sink. The bottles and tube get rinsed in cool, clean water, then are set out to air-dry. We lift the wine container onto the top of the tall trash can in the kitchen. Previously the wine sat undisturbed all summer in the pantry with an occasional "barrel" tasting to make sure it would really be worth all this trouble.

I attach one end of the tubing to the spigot; the other goes into the neck of a bottle. I hold on tight and open the valve. I've not chosen the best of places to conduct this procedure, as I can't see how quickly the wine rises in the bottle. Too dark down there on the floor with a dark brown-green glass bottle even though the lights are turned on. It is after sundown, after all.

Unexpectedly (yet expected all the same) the bottle overflows. There is cursing, more spillage, and hands and fingers that are not fast enough. This happens over and over again as the bottles get filled, a puddle of ruby liquid at my feet. My fingers are saturated with wine, and I lap at my hands (I contemplate licking the floor) because I don't want to lose one bit. The wine tastes good. Not perfect, not interesting, but good. I am completely surprised, unbelieving, so I want to keep tasting to be sure. The wine is light and clean. Given the problems I had earlier with the pretty bacteria, I figure this is one of those small tragedies converted into a miracle. The wine bottles, varied in shape, stand tall and look like they are marching across the floor toward to the door and the wine racks in the barn where they will fine and settle for as long as they last.

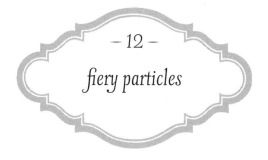

'Tis strange the mind, that very fiery particle . . .

Lord Byron

*M*y father is a consummate storyteller. He could
write great novels, or memoirs, but rather he has
saved his tales just for family. When I was still very young,
my father laid out before me stories of my family history,
stories of comic relief and cautionary wisdom. Around the
dining table my father would unroll his intricately woven
tales of being a young boy in a grand house during the
Depression, or the adventures he'd had as a young man
courting my mother. Every night when my family gathered for dinner—my mother and father, my two sisters,
and myself—my father would wend his way from the
day's current events to the saga of our Irish ancestors. His
stories were well seasoned with a mixture of high comedy,
Gothic mystery, and descriptions of family members and
friends that were always a little out of true. My sisters
and I would oblige him by asking questions and making
requests. We never tired of hearing the same stories more
than once. There was always another layer to be uncov-
ered, a new detail. I am so familiar with these stories now,
it is as if they are my own memories, their images distinct

and brightly colored, his narratives entwined so thoroughly with my own.

Since the dining room was my father's stage, perhaps this is why I have always loved the trappings of a meal. The house where I grew up was a white-painted brick Cape in southern Indiana not far from the Ohio River. It had a small but formal dining room in which we ate dinner every night. This room's elegance emanated from its molded chair rail, its ceiling trim painted Williamsburg blue, and its blue-and-white French toile wallpaper printed with curious birds cavorting between looping vines. A pewter chandelier hung over a long, well-waxed oval dining table whose many extra leaves could make ample room for guests. Circling this table were art-deco-style wooden chairs upholstered with a red-and-cream-striped Italian fabric. A sideboard flanking one wall held pewter candlesticks from New Orleans and an English silver coffee service, a gift from my father's mother. One wall was a bank of windows that looked out over my mother's garden full of camellias, sweet red honeysuckle, and white impatiens. A little red barn shaded by a big, muscular oak drew the eye out into the distance.

A brass bird cage that hung in a corner of the dining room housed Danny Boy, our lime-green parrot from Venezuela named after the melancholy song by the very Irish Clancy Brothers. He had a fine mastery of the English language. His most frequent phrase was "Damn it, Skeeter! Get off the table!" Skeeter was our naughty striped tabby cat, the only male among six cats who wandered in and out of our house. Somehow Danny Boy had captured the timbre and cadence of my mother's voice, and my sisters and I always laughed into our napkins when Danny Boy spoke. He chose the most opportune moments—during that lull in every conversation—usually when we were entertaining guests. In another corner of the room sat a small bar with a silver ice bucket and tongs, an empty decanter, and two bottles of ever-present liquor: Irish whisky and Scotch.

In my mind's eye, the bottle of Irish whisky was, and always will be, Jameson's. A green bottle with a cream-colored label with black and red writing. My father tells me this isn't true. My parents were always on the hunt for Murphy's, their favorite, and sometimes they drank Tullamore Dew. Jameson's was their default brand, and if they couldn't rustle up any of their preferred brands, they would turn to Bushmills, but really only in a worst-case scenario.

I always assumed that my parents took their evening cocktail—an Irish whisky on the rocks with a splash—because my father's parents drank Irish whisky, too, and had passed on the tradition. My father, however, tells me this also isn't true. My grandfather didn't drink in public, and while he was living neither did my grandmother. She would have a small sherry in the evening before my grand-father got home from work. There was almost never wine at the table. Only on Sundays at my great-granddad's house, a brooding Tudor-style affair, did the family, dressed in their finest, gather for lunch and to drink Champagne. We have a painting of my father in his Sunday lunch uniform: an Eton jacket and Buster Brown collar. The children drank ginger ale in Champagne glasses and got to sit at the big table in the dining room, unless Aunt Bernice and Uncle Don came, when there wouldn't be enough room. In that event, card tables dressed in linen would be set up for those under the age of twelve.

My grandmother had great élan. After my grandfather died, she was rather independent: smoking cigarettes, managing her own finances, and traveling around the world. As a widow, she took to bourbon (defiantly she seemed to drink this) and later switched to white wine after her doctor told her she shouldn't drink because of her health. I well remember her drinking her double bourbons on the rocks, looking dignified and swank in a sheared fur coat. She wintered in Florida and dressed for occasions. She was frighteningly direct, and not the most diplomatic companion. She suffered some deeply entrenched phobias. Her irrational fear of cats always proved stressful when she came to visit our house, as one or two of our half dozen resident felines inevitably chose her lap for a nap.

Even though my father's family is Irish-centric, no one seems to have chosen Irish whisky, except my parents, and that was for romantic reasons. In 1964, two years before I was born, my parents and two sisters took a summer sojourn in Ireland. My father, as acting headmaster at a private school in New Orleans, had the summers off. He planned their holiday for July and August, when it would ostensibly be the warmest season on the island. They rented a cottage on the bay in the village of Skull in the south. The tensions between the north of Ireland and the south were strong, and building—this was when the ancient animosity erupted into what the Irish call The

Troubles. I grew up with the feud between the Protestants and the Catholics in Ireland hovering overhead like a dark cloud. My parents read books by Leon Uris, and I remember sitting with my mother looking at the famous photo essay on war-torn Ireland that Uris wrote with his wife, Jill, who had taken all the photographs. The book is called *Ireland: A Terrible Beauty*. The angry, dirty faces of children, distorted by hatred, are still strong in my mind.

My mother had never traveled across the ocean until this journey in '64, and she decided she should go to confession the afternoon before they were to leave America. She stopped into St. Catherine of Siena, the church just a few blocks from their house in New Orleans, and sat in the pew at the front of the nave collecting her thoughts before going in to speak to her priest. A man sat at the back of the nave. When the priest called her into the confessional, she left her purse on the pew, a little woven raffia bag with a hinged top like a lunch box. In the bag, she had everything they would need for traveling the next day, a Sunday. After her confession, she came out to collect her belongings, but her purse was gone, along with the four passports inside. The man who had been sitting at the back of the church had disappeared.

My mother says my father was furious. My father doesn't say much about that, just relates how the event unleashed an incredible chain of events. He called my grandmother, who was in the midst of hosting a cocktail party (yes, this was after my grandfather had passed away). She knew a man who had been very high up in Roosevelt's administration—he was perhaps even the secretary of commerce at some point—and this Mr. Sawyer provided names and direct numbers for my father to call.

My father talked to a woman, who told him what he needed to do in order to get new passports on short notice, a Herculean task. My parents were able to collect the required duplicates of their health certificates from their doctor. They interrupted his evening Mardi Gras Krewe meeting. Being a sympathetic man, he was willing to open up his office and make the copies. They found a photo booth at a traveling carnival on the outskirts of town in order to procure the small photos needed for their documents, though they were unsure if these would qualify, as usually one had to provide a certified photograph that would then be stapled into the passport.

They flew the next morning to New York City as planned, but had to delay their flight a day in order to wait for the US embassy to open on Monday to issue the new passports. They flew out Monday night, already exhausted from the hustle and uncertainty of the last twenty-four hours.

My mother tells me that a year later, in the late summer of 1965 after Hurricane Betsy (the worst hurricane to hit New Orleans before Katrina arrived), the priest from St. Catherine of Siena called her to say that the storm had unearthed a woven straw bag with her identification inside. They'd found the purse in the church's boiler room, missing nothing but the five dollars my mother had had in her wallet. The passports were untouched. The man at the back of the church on that day was known to the parish priest as someone who was always desperate for his next drink. The five dollars was enough to help him along.

My mother and father have always been attracted to the finer things, and whenever they had the means to obtain them, they would do so. The year 1964 was a good one for my family, and my father loved the idea of arriving in Dublin and staying at the old Shelbourne Hotel, replete with its Grand Tour lobby. Its chambermaids still wore neatly pressed black serge uniforms and white aprons.

Within the first few days of arriving in Dublin, my family attended the Dublin Horse Show, one of the great international competitions. Like me, my father inclines toward the romantic, and he had managed to get two tickets to the Hunt Ball being held at the Shelbourne during the horse show. My parents had grown up in an age of cotillions and holiday balls at which my father wore a top hat and tails, and my mother donned one of a handful of very elegant gowns, the well-made fabric just long enough to whisper across the floor. Living in New Orleans afforded them the opportunity to dress for Mardi Gras balls, and they loved the notion of packing their fancy dress for a party three thousand miles away. My mother had brought with her a long ivory gown with thin straps that she wore with long white kid-leather opera gloves. My father had packed his classic shawl-collared tuxedo. My sisters, at the ages of six and nine, too young to attend yet smitten with the story of Cinderella, were not pleased to be banned from the festivities. Images of pretty women in chic ball gowns and gallant men gliding across the floor danced before their eyes. In an effort to placate their children, my parents bought two incredibly intricate marionettes for my sisters to play with that evening: two characters from *The Wizard of Oz,* another story that had captured my sisters' imaginations—Glenda, the Good Witch of the North, and poor, ruined green Elphaba, the Wicked Witch of the West, almost distracted them. However, the young chambermaid who watched after them fretted that she would lose them every time they ran out of the hotel room to the balcony to try to catch a glimpse of the party.

To travel out of Dublin, my family had rented a small Volkswagen Beetle, my father thinking it would be the same car that he drove at home. He'd forgotten that he would need to quickly learn to reverse his driving skills. They carefully drove to the village of Skull and set up house in the little white cottage that would be theirs for the summer. The cottage looked out over the bay, and the beach was just down the street. On the main floor, the house boasted a cozy living room with a peat fire in the fireplace, a dining room, and a kitchen. Up a central staircase, bedrooms hid under the eaves.

They settled into a daily routine of looking for cockle shells on the beach, or pony trekking at Mr. Sweeney's, outings that frightened my mother, her fears enhanced by her belief that Mr. Sweeney was not a very nice man. She was appalled by his roughness with the ponies, his short temper with her daughters, and his overly sharp, pointed features. She remembers his face looking like the edge of a razor, or a particularly wily rat.

Cooking in Ireland provided a challenge for my mother. She found the gaminess of the mutton, beef, and poultry difficult for her palate and stomach. In a panic from the overtly earthy flavors she was not accustomed to, she found a small grocery that carried Birdseye products, and reluctantly relied on canned and frozen vegetables. Then she discovered that the family that helped caretake the cottage had a bountiful garden. For the rest of the summer, my parents and sisters dined simply on fresh tomatoes, lettuces, potatoes, and local fish. When they traveled in the countryside, they would eat the plentiful fresh salmon.

In the evenings, my parents would go to the local pub. The first night they arrived, they had stopped in to get their bearings, to get a feel for their new community. My father had gone up to the bartender to ask for two Scotch on the rocks. The bartender replied, "When you're in Ireland, you drink Irish whisky. Will you be having a Murphy's then?" My father immediately understood his mistake and enthusiastically agreed to the local choice. Just like the other locals, my parents came to the pub out of habit most evenings for their drink and chat. Occasionally there would be country dances with fiddlers and banjo players, groups of men and women dancing a jig. On such nights, laughter and shouting intermingled with the smell of sweat, whisky, and peat smoke.

It was here in Skull, with its scent of salt on the air, and the whistle of wind about the houses, that my parents fell in love with Ireland. The taste of the whisky defined it ever after. Murphy's Irish whisky would always conjure a bittersweet nostalgia. It would become a souvenir of a well-remembered, happy time in their life.

Some days that summer they would go out on excursions, and once they drove up the coast to the north where my father's family originated. They stopped along the way to take a boat out to the Isle of Innisfree, a pilgrimage that my father, a great fan of Yeats, felt he had to make. They saw the cabin that "clay and wattles" made, and stood in the "bee-loud glade." Many years later, my oldest sister would read the poem "The Lake Isle of Innisfree" at my grandmother's funeral, the coffin covered in a blanket of yellow roses, remembering the boat ride across the water when she was just nine years old.

On the way north, the four stopped in Bundoren, where there was a family hotel high on a cliff overlooking a blue-green sea. My sisters, according to my parents, could be rather adventurous and naughty (my adult sisters protest). My father and mother remember seeing a poster for a local fair, and while they were unpacking and not looking, my sisters followed the signs and ran away to the carnival. I can imagine them gawking at a bearded lady and trying to sneak onto the rides. Once my parents discovered that their daughters were gone, they feared the children had slipped and fallen from the serpentine path. This steep trail was cut into the side of the cliff that led down from the hotel to the beach. My parents called and looked everywhere. A few hours later, my sisters returned of their own accord, their faces smudged with something sticky like candy and dirty like soot, looking like mischievous gypsies. They were confined for the rest of the evening to the hotel room. They begged  to be allowed to go out on the balcony for some fresh air. There they spent the hours before bedtime spitting down on the heads of hotel guests below, taking careful aim at the tops of their pates for ten points each. This went on until my parents understood the girls' supposed fascination with watching the sun set over the water.

On this excursion north, all four dressed in their new thick sun-bleached Irish sweaters and plaid scarves, even though it was August. On damp nights, the inns where they stopped would warm the beds with copper bedwarmers filled with coals of smoldering peat. Luxuriant at first, the heat would dissipate within five minutes, and my family slept huddled together under as many blankets as the inn could spare. When they arrived in the village of Malenbeg in Donegal, a town of about ten cottages with stuccoed walls and thatched roofs, my parents went to the nearest post office to inquire after relatives. There they saw a small child with red hair, freckles, and an urchiny look in her eye dawdling by the counter. The postmistress proved to be little help, but the girl, who was about my eldest sister's age at the time, said her mother was a Heekin, a Mary Ellen Heekin Duggan, and offered to lead them to her, and also to a Mr. John Heekin who lived in the village. She was as good as her promise. John Heekin, who lived in one of the cottages, with a well-swept dirt floor, was a master of many trades. He farmed a large garden, raised sheep for wool and meat, and did whatever jobs he could find. He lived in exactly the same way that my great-great-grandfather had a hundred years earlier, the only difference being that in 1964 there was no potato famine, and the villagers were not starving. My great-great-grandfather was a man whom I idolized, for he and I shared the same birth date, and he had made a brave journey across the ocean to a foreign land. He was an émigré, and somehow this notion of his rootlessness appealed to me and would inform my own journeys across the same ocean.

The people in my ancestral village were very kind to my parents and sisters, showing them a cottage along the road that they said had been my father's great-grandfather's house. It was well kept and had been modernized with a shingle roof. My father took a picture and had it framed when they returned Stateside, a picture I remember well in its narrow gilt frame. It hung on a hallway wall, the photo offset by a French matte with a Gaelic-style script below naming it: *The Heekin Cottage in Malenbeg, Donegal.* The photograph itself was washed out by light; it was easy to see it had been a sunny, summer-sky kind of day. I imagined this was a house to which I myself could one day return. It wasn't until I was much older, grown and living under my own roof, that my father revealed his suspicions that this wasn't his ancestors' cottage at all, but the house that the locals showed to all returning relatives to make them feel good about their origins.

My family returned to New Orleans at the end of the summer, feeling windswept and carefree, the best effect a summer holiday can have. My parents kept up their evening ritual of the Irish whisky before dinner, having brought a bottle of Murphy's back with them. They drank their memories at home in New Orleans, not in a local Irish pub where stout matrons and freshly shaved farmers would dance the night away. After that souvenir bottle was gone, my parents always searched for Murphy's and would buy as many bottles as they could whenever they found it, because at that time it was only this flavor that allowed them to relive their summer in Ireland.

In September 1964, the school year started, as did the long preparations for Mardi Gras. By the next hurricane season, they were boarding up their little house on Sycamore Street and hunkering down against the violent winds of disastrous Betsy. Shortly after Mardi Gras of 1966, my mother was pregnant with me, and at the end of that summer at home, my mother having a difficult pregnancy, my family would move. They would head north, but stay south—still on a river, still on a delta, still worried about crumbling levees. I was born in Evansville, Indiana, south of Louisville, and only two hours north of Nashville. It wouldn't be until forty years later that I would make my first trip to Ireland, following the trail of Irish whisky.

My husband and I arrived in the small airport in Belfast on a beautiful spring evening. We always seem to be arriving, my husband and I. I prefer always to note the arriving, and not to think so much about the departing. I am drawn by the promise that arriving holds. The leaving for me is always sad; it is like the conclusion of a great meal, the end of a great bottle of wine, or the empty fairgrounds after the carnival has gone. Endings must shape any story, yet I choose to lavish my focus on the beginnings.

This was the first time my husband and I had come to visit Ireland, our travels having always taken us to the Continent before. This would be a short visit, one to whet the appetite. On this trip, there would not be enough time to go to my family's village of Malenbeg, the original purpose of our stopover. Instead, we would spend a few days with friends who had just bought an apartment in a fishing village in the north outside Belfast. We would make a list of things to do the next time we came.

The North. It felt strange that my first visit to my country of origin was, as I might say, across enemy lines. Just recently in the news, a truce had been declared by the warring factions in Belfast. In Belfast, I am shocked to learn that the Catholics and Protestants live cheek by jowl, that a great iron wall separates the two sections of the city, and that on weekends a gate is closed, and there is a curfew. Of course, that doesn't stop angry rebels from throwing crude homemade bombs over the wall. Though, to be fair, it has been a while since the tensions have been that taut.

Since my knowledge of The Troubles is based on murky, angry photographs and relatives who secretly gave money to the IRA, my husband and I decide to take a Black Taxi Tour of Belfast to get our history straight. You can hire a Black Taxi—a 1950s black-painted taxi with red interior—to drive around the two opposing sections of the city. Our friend Susan suspects that the driver is Irish Catholic, and there is a strange dance around several seemingly meaningless topics of conversation. When the driver understands that Susan is from north of Belfast, he tries to get a gauge of her beliefs. One way is centered on the pronunciation of my very Irish name. The driver asks me how I pronounce it, which I find strange since here we are in the place where my name originates and has real meaning. I answer that in my family we say *deer-dra*. Susan quickly adds that I am from the United States, and she is sure I don't mind if my name is pronounced *deer-dra* or the

English *deer-dree.* I understand from her expression that it is important I agree. It becomes clear later that this simple way of pronouncing either a soft, short *a* at the end of my name, or a long *ee,* tells volumes of a story that I don't fully understand. *A* means that you are Irish Catholic, and *ee* means that you are Protestant and a descendant from the English or the Scots. Depending on whom you are speaking with, a change in pronunciation could cause a heated argument, or even a threat of danger.

Our driver takes us down Shankhill. On this road are the Protestant or Orange projects of the city. A series of cheaply made low-slung apartment buildings surround a series of greens. On walls facing the greensward, the inhabitants have painted a collection of evocative murals. A man with a ski mask, army camouflage, and a rifle is shown in such a perspective that he seems to have both his eyes and his gun trained on you at all times. Another mural depicts the landing of William of Orange on Irish shores. What I know of William of Orange is that he tried to starve, infect, and oust the already resident Catholics.

We actually get out of the car and walk around to see the paintings. Susan and the driver both say it is completely safe, though it is difficult to not feel curious eyes, the hostile eyes of that mural, and the strange sensation of being in a war zone whose cease-fire rocks on a precarious balance. We see the start of piles of refuse for bonfires. Soon it will be time for the Orange Fires, when the Protestants in Shankhill light their pyres and march across the city, showcasing their pride. This is a time when most Catholics and neutral Protestants stay indoors.

On the way to the Catholic neighborhood, we drive along the wall separating the two factions. Thousands upon thousands have written on the wall, pleading for peace and creating a kaleidoscopic graffiti that swirls around the outline of a massive dove. The driver hands me a felt-tip pen. I get out of the taxi and find a blank space among all these written prayers. In thick black letters, I write a simple phrase: HERE'S TO THE DOVE. I sign my full, very Irish Catholic name, DEIRDRE MOLLOY HEEKIN, and date it. I walk slowly back to the taxi, feeling the weight of all that has gone on here.

The Catholic side is much different. The neighborhood is defined by mews houses in a new brick, the result of development money paid out after the Protestants destroyed the previous housing in the neighborhood. The streets and buildings look well kept and prosperous, with crisp lace curtains in the windows and fresh, thriving flowers in the window boxes. There is a small cemetery with names listed of the people who have died in the countless skirmishes between the two sides, and one mural looks out at us, a dark and bloody tale of violent events. As we pass out of the neighborhood, we see another mural depicting the Hunger Strikers of the seventies, led by Bobby Sands who died for Irish independence. They look out at us with sad but fighting eyes, forever captured in their youth.

Susan tells us that the strife of this feud is mostly felt in Belfast itself, and that growing up in a small town on the seaside north of the city, she was mostly unaware of what was going on. Her family, descended from Scottish Presbyterians, found the whole affair incredibly distasteful and overwrought. It's true, however, that in her village, as in the countless pretty and peaceful towns that we drive through, we would never guess what had transpired over the centuries.

We decide to drive north. We are going to the Bushmills Distillery. Again, I feel a small sense of betrayal because I know that Bushmills is a Protestant whisky, but I haven't seen Murphy's anywhere, and I want to learn about what defines *whisky.* Not unlike my parents, I'll take what I can get. I also begin to feel that there is purpose in stepping into the other side's shoes. I wonder: If Irish Catholic descendants of my generation were to come back to their homeland, but come to the north and see the beauty of the land and architecture, and experience the kindness of the people, would they turn the whole argument on its head? I realize my wish is idealistic and naïve. I don't believe that these age-old wars will ever die.

Our drive is met by brilliant sunshine, green fields flecked with white sheep, sweet stuccoed cottages clad with roses. The town of Bushmills is made up of Tudor-style buildings and a cozy pub and inn where we stop for lunch and eat delicious blood pudding and fish-and-chips. The blood pudding is nothing like I expect. I imagined something along the lines of an overly juicy French black sausage, yet Irish blood pudding is dry and cake-like. Its salty, earthy flavors are slightly sweet, and its texture is granular.

The distillery is a large property. As we walk into the main building, we can see farmers unloading trucks of fresh barley. The scent on the air is fermented and sweet, and we wonder if we can get drunk on the smell alone. We play tourist and sign up for the official tour, which begins with a short film on the history of Irish whisky.

The word *whisky* is an Anglicization of the Gaelic *uisce beatha,* which means "water of life." Catholic monks had traveled to the Middle East during the Crusades in the Middle Ages and discovered the Arabian alembic, a chemical apparatus with a wide bottom, and *retorts,* or beakers with long glass necks, that could fully purify chemicals. The alembic is the precursor to what we think of as the pot still. The Babylonians in Mesopotamia (what is now known as Iraq) used these early types of alembics, or early forms for making essential oils and perfumes, as long ago as the second millennium BC.

In Pakistan, archaeological excavations show that the distillation of alcohol has been around since 500 BC. Greek alchemists practiced distillation in the first century AD. But distillation as we think of it today, distillation by alembic, was developed by Arabic and Persian chemists in the eighth century. They refined distillation in order to produce both esters, or perfumes, and pure alcohol. Jabir ibn Hayyan was the first to be credited with the invention of what we think of as the modern alembic. The isolation of ethanol, or alcohol, as a pure chemical compound was first achieved by the Arab chemist al-Kindi. Petroleum was first distilled by the Persian chemist Muhammad ib Zakariva Razi in the ninth century in order to produce kerosene; and Avicenna, the Persian polymath—physician, philosopher, astronomer, chemist, geologist, logician, paleontologist, mathematician, physicist, poet, psychologist, scientist, sheikh, soldier, statesman, teacher, and Islamic theologian—invented steam distillation in the early eleventh century. This method produced essential oils for perfumes. Perfumes and alcohol—the two seem to be forever influencing each other, and allied.

As the works of Middle Eastern scribes began to move across the globe, distillation became a part of alchemy in India. Then it was introduced to medieval Europe through Latin translations of Arabic chemical treatises. By the 1500s, European alchemists were publishing manuscripts solely on the art of distillation.

The Irish monks, who had been brewing beer already for centuries, could see the next step of refinement in their process. They packed up an Arabian alembic on an old mule and brought it back to the monastery. It was here that they began to experiment first with maceration and fermentation, then with distilling their barley wine.

The tour guide takes us through the physical distill-ery with its huge copper alembics built from that origi-nal model that came back from Arabian deserts. He talks about the three processes of distillation. The first is the maceration and fermentation that produce the barley wine; then this wine is distilled, and the impurities—the unwanted compounds known as the heads and tails—are discarded from the liquid;   then another distillation further strengthens the wine and increases its alcoholic fire. After distillation, the whisky is contained, stored, and aged in various types of wood for varying lengths of time. The whiskies at Bushmills are aged in barrels previously used to make American bourbon, Spanish oloroso sherry, and Madeira wine. The woods and their previous liqueurs bring out various attributes in the whisky and develop certain kinds of flavors.

When the tour guide asks for a volunteer, I automatically raise my hand. My friends tease me that I must have been that annoying student who sat at the front of class and wanted to answer every question. I think of this more as volunteering for a magic show, and I vaguely wonder if the magician will try to cut me in half.

I have volunteered to be a Master Taster. Three of us in the group will get to taste all the whiskies that Bushmills makes. We adjourn to the Tasting Room. On the way, we walk across a bridge in the bottling plant and see that not only Bushmills bottles are being filled, capped, and labeled, but also the southern Irish brand Jameson's.

The tour guide brings us several different tastes of the whisky in little glasses. The whiskies all have varying degrees of concentration and smoothness. There is Bushmills Original, a blend of single-malt made from 100 percent malted barley distilled in a pot still, and grain whisky made from grains distilled in a column still. The grain whisky is matured in American oak casks. Generally, grain whisky tastes much lighter and more neutral in flavor than single-malt and is almost never bottled as a single grain. It is instead used to combine with single-malt to produce a lighter blended whisky. We taste Black Bush, a blend comprising mostly single-malts, originally developed in 1934. Its malt is matured in selected Spanish oloroso-sherry-seasoned oak casks before it is blended with delicate sweet single-grain whisky. Bushmills ten-year-old single-malt is matured in American bourbon barrels for at least ten years, and Bushmills twelve-year single-malt, a special edition currently sold only at the Bushmills Distillery, is matured mostly in sherry casks.

The tour guide brings us another treat: a Scotch whisky to taste in order to compare the styles. The Scotch is so peaty and smoky, having been cured with peat fire, that it makes an astounding contrast with the sweet spices of the Irish style. I get a shiver up my spine.

It's clear that the young whiskies are not as elegant and have sharper edges to the taste. The twelve-year-old Bushmills captures my fancy. It is buttery, almost like caramel in the nose, and the first mouthful tastes like fiery particles breaking up over my tongue. Then a hint of malt follows. After, a lasting finish of crushed almonds, and even sweet marzipan.

The distillery offers a special option for those interested: They will label a bottle of the twelve-year-old whisky with our names if we like. And here we are playing tourist. I have just received my certificate proclaiming me as a Master Taster for the Bushmills Distillery. My cheeks feel ruddy, the taste of almonds still lingering on my tongue. *Why not?* we think. How sweet will that be to arrive at home and have a taste of our very own twelve-year-old Irish whisky already waiting for us? We'll toast and remember our trip here to the north of Ireland.

I feel like my parents, dancing at the Hunt Ball, or watching the country jigs whirling around the pub to the sound of a fiddle, or coming home from their own journey in 1964 with their bottle of Murphy's tucked safely in their suitcase—the same bottle that they tasted slowly, and saved for special occasions so as not to finish it too fast. They knew how difficult this whisky would be to find in our country.

My parents bottled up their memories of their Irish summer, and, like them, I have bottled memories of every journey I've taken, in bottles of rare varietal wine, or dark, thick *amaro,* or a clear vodka scented with bison grass, or this sweet barley whisky from the shores of my origin.

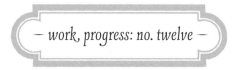

— *work, progress: no. twelve* —

*Probasti me et chognuisti me*
"Try me and know me." A motto in ancient
Piemontese dialect found on the label of an old wine bottle

As I write this, I imagine a wind and a specific day not long past: Hurricane Ike sent his fierce tailwinds up to us from the Gulf. He had already devastated Houston, but gone light on New Orleans. In the deep center of the night, at about two o'clock in the morning, the air and the sky were perfectly still. Our bedroom window was wide open, and a bright moon shone down. I was hoping the official predictions for sixty-mile-an-hour winds would never come to fruition, that Ike's wildness would bypass Vermont entirely. Then I saw our two black cats slowly approach the window, their heads held high, sniffing at the air. I could detect no changes myself, but within two minutes a breeze began to ruffle the leaves on the trees. Wispy clouds rolled in, and the bright moon was suddenly gone as if someone had just snuffed out a light. I could hear a big wind, a serious wind, rolling down through the wild forest of the Chateauguay. This wind sounded like the ebb and flow of a rough surf. I closed the window. Weather began pummeling the house, and this wind continued pushing and gusting at our windows and doors all night. The floors and roof creaked, our house lamenting.

I was up most of the night, held awake by the sound. The next evening, or maybe I must now call it this evening as the clock is well past midnight, we have scheduled a celebration at the house, a wine tasting for fifty to launch the new label and concept of our restaurant gardens and vineyard. I have named this project La Garagista after the avant-garde French winemakers in the eighties who made small-batch wines with the best of that year's harvest in their barns and garages. Les Garagistes made big, extracted, modern wines with great character in small spaces at very little expense as a response to the notion that you need millions of dollars to make an exemplary wine. Many of the Garagistes wines are now the most sought-after in the world. While I follow in their footsteps making "garage wine," I want to twist the shape of their idea to fit my own. I will make wine in the old way with as little intervention as possible, and once my own grapes can be used, almost all of my work will happen in the vineyard rather than the cellar.

There is also another layer to my choice of name for our work here on our property. The first raised beds of our vegetable gardens were planted within the confines of a sunken stone wall on the site of our old garage. When we bought our property ten years ago, an unfortunate summer "camp" (an uninsulated structure) in an open meadow with a stunning view, the garage was the most attractive building. Over the years, as we modified and rebuilt the house, the garage slowly became the ugliest and least functional structure. We toasted with Champagne on the foggy winter day when Caleb took down the last wall of that garage, and we will toast again on this night that ghostly garage that now will give place to so many new possibilities. Not only are the garden beds lined with the cedar from the walls and roof of that demolished garage, but Caleb built a series of rustic wine-tasting tables from the salvaged wood that we will use for this night's party and future events. That garage has taught us so much, but mostly the lesson that, in what we perceive as ugliness, true grace is hidden.

Just yesterday, Caleb helped me hang the sign I designed that says LA GARAGISTA on the new garage, which is really a small carriage barn. The sign is suspended by a brawny, sinewy piece of old wild grapevine that we found on the property. As we worked to get ready, I wondered if the remnants of Ike's rage would make our evening's festivities impossible.

That morning the sky cleared, but the wind still howled and pressed. The bean trellis had been blown down, its old wood covered in a tangle of green leaves and vine. We expected this. We went about our chores as if the evening would come off without a snag. We'd been collecting and arranging flowers, setting up tables, procuring the food, setting out wineglasses. Would it rain? Would it be too windy?

The outlook for the day improved. We ate a take-out lunch on the porch, the wind nearly spent. We felt almost confident and at ease. Our celebration would happen. People would come. We would open bottles of wine. We would share the harvest together.

I set up the sign-in table in the barn. We had spent months cleaning and organizing this space. One wall was lined with stacked firewood for winter, next to a wine rack filled with bottles. The floor was dirt, but in the center stood one of our wine-tasting tables set with glasses and an old French-style candelabrum that is very elegant. Light poured in through the narrow, long windows. Our friends Mark and Gina had loaned me a copper wine trough that we filled with ice and water and bottles of a sparkling rosé that would usher in the evening. Iacopo, Rafael, and Winthrop, our friends who would show the ten wines we'd be featuring, opened and tasted the bottles, then lined them on the table in the stone garden.

Iacopo, our friend from Italy, would be representing the importer of these wines. Rafael owns the small company that brings them to us here in Vermont. Winthrop has recently started to work with Rafael. Michael, another friend volunteering for the evening, joined Caleb to set up the *bruschetteria,* and began to tend to the big open fire on which to toast the bread for the myriad toppings they have prepared. Caleb's mother, Carol, lighted a small fire in a galvanized metal tub, our version of a fire pit, so people could warm themselves in the stone garden as the evening cooled. Cousin Claire, and our friends Anthony and Christy, lit all the torches and candles. Conversation and laughter bubbled around the house and barn, and we felt as if we had dodged the wicked weather until five twenty-five. Five minutes before guests were to arrive, clouds crested the hill above, and it began to rain. *Oh, well,* I thought, *what a shame. We'll just have to stuff everyone in the barn.* No one spoke.

But then, like a tease, the rain stopped, and the clouds thinned out into mare's tails. There was a collective sigh, and a couple of people laughed away the tension. Guests began to arrive. The energy was high.

It turned out to be a beautiful evening. The wines were sublime and showed themselves to be elegant, gallant, coy, and charming—the perfect hosts. The tastes that Caleb and Michael offered were lively and married the wines well. Guests walked through the gardens, sitting and contemplating or conversing. We all watched the moon rise, a fantastic harvest moon. No one really noticed the downed bean trellis that never got rebuilt during the course of the day, there not being enough time.

Now, after all the guests have left, fifteen of us, a combination of family and friends who helped coordinate the evening, stay for dinner. We line four of the tasting tables down the center of the barn. Someone accidentally knocks over a bottle of open wine. The wine spills and puddles on the wood, and I think how perfectly it christens this table for our first of what I hope will be many dinners in this barn. We set the long table with fine china and silver and the two Baroque candelabra. We pull chairs from around the property and inside the house. We set up a buffet to serve a *purea* of zucchini and onion soup made from ingredients in the garden, and plates of a silky, sliced, local pork belly seasoned with wine and sage, served with small, pearl white beans. On the table are plates of oysters to begin, a gift brought by a friend, and the last of the bruschetta. Countless bottles of wine have been opened, and everyone tastes and retastes the stars of the evening. Iacopo has brought the last of a wine made from a cru selection of grapes that he helped make in Tuscany; and I open local winemaker Chris Granstrom's Cove Road made from Marquette, St. Croix, and Frontenac. We toast and congratulate each other for an evening well done.

It is time to open the first bottle of my own first vintage made from grapes all the way from Italy. A true "garage wine." The glass is plain, recycled from a bottle of my favorite Aglianico made in Campania. I'm hopeful that the bottle, once the home of a great wine, will elevate my own effort. Iacopo teases me because, on the handwritten label I have hung around the neck, I have written *La Garagista, Vintage No. 1, 2008.* "What do you mean 2008?" he asks. Flustered, I take my pen, cross out the *8*, and write in a *7*. I am jumping ahead of myself. I haven't even received my juice for this year's vintage yet. (Patience has never been one of my virtues. Is impatience the vice of any young winemaker?)

I uncork, and we pour. I'm nervous that my wine may have turned to vinegar. We taste. While my first endeavor is simple with a soft finish, it's smooth with the flavors of red currant and warm, sweet spices. Acidity and tannic structure do not yet show themselves. But this wine is only a year old, made from grapes that make a wine that gets better as it gets older. Aloud, I deem it just drinkable. We all laugh, then everyone kindly becomes silent, a reverence that is about the work behind the bottle, not about whether this wine is good or not. Quality is no longer important. This moment has become about continuity, about practicing the ongoing and ancient art of making wine, about allowing ourselves to be defined by our senses and the perceptions of the world around us. This moment is about the alchemy of our memory of this evening, how a dangerous wind in the future might bring us back to this candlelit table in our barn. The scent and aroma of bright red currants and hints of spice like cinnamon and star anise will someday provide a doorway through which any one of the fifteen of us can walk. We can escape to an evening defined by the scents and tastes of food and wine, by a storm averted, by companionship and conversation and a harvest moon. This is the true meaning and success of alchemy: the necessary magic of memory.

# — acknowledgments —

Many thanks go to all those who helped bring this book to fruition. Thank you to R. and C. for always visiting the restaurant on your Valentine's wedding anniversary, and for asking about the next book. Thank you to Margo and Ian for coming to the restaurant for the first time on Valentine's Day and ". . . overhearing the conversation at the next table . . ." Thank you to all the St. Valentines, worthy martyrs of ancient Rome, heretics and believers in chance, without whom none of this would have happened. Thank you to my agent Marian Young for believing in this project. Thank you to friends and family who encouraged. Thank you to all my unsung mentors and inspirations, for they are many. Thank you to Margaret Edwards for valiant friendship, guidance, and the countless, tedious hours of reading and correcting. Thank you to my editor Ben Watson for his meticulous eye and expertise, and other readers who kept me from straying off the path. Thank you to everyone at Chelsea Green who pulled the project together and nudged it out the door. Thank you to Claire who gardened while I wrote. Thank you to Jamey, who inspired this journey in the first place. Mostly, thank you to my husband, Caleb, who made a litany out of cups of espresso, green tea, cocktails, glasses of wine, and beautiful meals with which to break the work.

"This logo identifies paper that meets the standards of the Forest Stewardship Council. FSC is widely regarded as the best practice in forest management, ensuring the highest protections for forests and indigenous peoples."

Chelsea Green Publishing is committed to preserving ancient forests and natural resources. We elected to print this title on 30-percent postconsumer recycled paper, processed chlorine-free. As a result, for this printing, we have saved:

**28 Trees (40' tall and 6-8" diameter)**
**10,169 Gallons of Wastewater**
**19 Million BTUs Total Energy**
**1,306 Pounds of Solid Waste**
**2,450 Pounds of Greenhouse Gases**

Chelsea Green Publishing made this paper choice because we and our printer, Thomson-Shore, Inc., are members of the Green Press Initiative, a nonprofit program dedicated to supporting authors, publishers, and suppliers in their efforts to reduce their use of fiber obtained from endangered forests. For more information, visit: www.greenpressinitiative.org.

Environmental impact estimates were made using the Environmental Defense Paper Calculator. For more information visit: www.papercalculator.org.

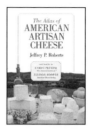

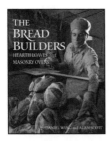
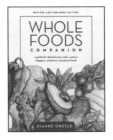